GCSE RELIGIOUS STUDIES FOR EDEXCEL B

Religion and Ethics

through Islam

Waqar Ahmad Ahmedi

OXFORD
UNIVERSITY·PRESS

OXFORD
UNIVERSITY PRESS

Great Clarendon Street, Oxford, OX2 6DP, United Kingdom

Oxford University Press is a department of the University of Oxford. It furthers the University's objective of excellence in research, scholarship, and education by publishing worldwide. Oxford is a registered trade mark of Oxford University Press in the UK and in certain other countries

British Library Cataloguing in Publication Data
Data available

978-0-19-837041-3

10 9 8 7 6 5 4 3 2

Paper used in the production of this book is a natural, recyclable product made from wood grown in sustainable forests. The manufacturing process conforms to the environmental regulations of the country of origin.

Printed in India by Multivista Global Pvt. Ltd

Links to third party websites are provided by Oxford in good faith and for information only. Oxford disclaims any responsibility for the materials contained in any third party website referenced in this work.

endorsed for
edexcel

In order to ensure that this resource offers high-quality support for the associated Pearson qualification, it has been through a review process by the awarding body. This process confirms that this resource fully covers the teaching and learning content of the specification or part of a specification at which it is aimed. It also confirms that it demonstrates an appropriate balance between the development of subject skills, knowledge and understanding, in addition to preparation for assessment.

Endorsement does not cover any guidance on assessment activities or processes (e.g. practice questions or advice on how to answer assessment questions), included in the resource nor does it prescribe any particular approach to the teaching or delivery of a related course.

While the publishers have made every attempt to ensure that advice on the qualification and its assessment is accurate, the official specification and associated assessment guidance materials are the only authoritative source of information and should always be referred to for definitive guidance.

Pearson examiners have not contributed to any sections in this resource relevant to examination papers for which they have responsibility.

Examiners will not use endorsed resources as a source of material for any assessment set by Pearson. Endorsement of a resource does not mean that the resource is required to achieve this Pearson qualification, nor does it mean that it is the only suitable material available to support the qualification, and any resource lists produced by the awarding body shall include this and other appropriate resources.

Thank you

I would like to express my deepest gratitude to everyone involved in the publication of this textbook, whom I have had the enormous privilege of working with:

- the fantastic team at Oxford University Press, for their help and support
- the faith reviewers, scholars and other teachers, for their important advice and guidance
- everyone featured in the case studies, for their invaluable contributions.

I must also pay tribute to my better half, Wajeeha, and our three children, Anam, Roshaan and Yusuf, for their remarkable forbearance – and, more importantly, undiminished love – while I slogged (and frequently hid myself) away during the research and writing for this project.

Without them all, this work would not have been possible. I very much hope that teachers and students find this resource informative, insightful and enriching.

Waqar Ahmad Ahmedi

From the publisher: OUP wishes to thank Shaykh Ibrahim Mogra for his help reviewing this book.

Contents

Edexcel GCSE Religious Studies 4

Exam skills 6

Introduction to Islam 12

Chapter 1:
Muslim Beliefs 14

1.1 The six Beliefs 16

1.2 The five roots of 'Usul ad-Din 19

1.3 The nature of Allah 21

1.4 Risalah 24

1.5 Muslim holy books 28

1.6 Malaikah 31

1.7 Al-Qadr 34

1.8 Akhirah 37

Revision and Exam Practice 41

Chapter 2:
Marriage and the Family 45

2.1 Marriage 47

2.2 Sexual relationships 49

2.3 The family 52

2.4 Support for the family 55

2.5 Contraception 59

2.6 Divorce 61

2.7 Equality of men and women 64

2.8 Gender prejudice and discrimination 67

Revision and Exam Practice 71

Chapter 3:
Living the Muslim Life 75

3.1 Ten Obligatory Acts 77

3.2 Shahadah 79

3.3 Salah 82

3.4 Sawm 85

3.5 Zakah and Khums 89

3.6 Hajj 92

3.7 Jihad 95

3.8 Celebrations and commemorations 98

Revision and Exam Practice 101

Chapter 4:
Matters of Life and Death 105

4.1 Origins and value of the universe 107

4.2 Sanctity of life 111

4.3 Origins and value of human life 113

4.4 Abortion 116

4.5 Life after death 119

4.6 Responses to arguments against life after death 122

4.7 Euthanasia 126

4.8 Issues in the natural world 129

Revision and Exam Practice 133

Glossary 137

Index 140

Edexcel GCSE Religious Studies

This book covers all you'll need to study for Edexcel GCSE Religious Studies Paper 1C: Religion and Ethics through Islam. Whether you're studying for the full course or the short course, this book will provide the knowledge you'll need, as well as plenty of opportunities to prepare for your GCSE examinations.

GCSE Religious Studies provides the opportunity to study a truly fascinating subject. The word 'divergence', which means separation or parting of the ways, is used a lot throughout the specification, and you will get the opportunity to debate big moral issues, understand and analyse a diverse range of opinions, as well as think for yourself about the meaning of life.

How is the specification covered?

- The Edexcel specification is split into **four sections**:
  – *Muslim Beliefs*
  – *Marriage and the Family*
  – *Living the Muslim Life*
  – *Matters of Life and Death*

This book has **four chapters**, which match these sections. If you are taking the short course, you will only need to cover the first two sections: *Muslim Beliefs*, and *Marriage and the Family*.

- Each of the four sections of the specification is split into **eight sub-sections**. These cover specific topics, like 'the nature of Allah', or 'divorce'. To support this, each chapter in this book is also split into the same eight sub-sections.

How to use this book

- So that you are fully prepared for your exams, you need to work through every chapter of this book (or just the first two for the short course). At the end of every topic there are exam-style questions which you should use to test your knowledge and practise your writing. Answering exam questions regularly, throughout your GCSE course, will really help you to be confident when exam time arrives.

- In the main topics there are lots of features to guide you through the material:

A **compare and contrast** feature appears in 1.8 and 3.3. On these topics in your exam you may be required to compare Muslim and Christian beliefs.

Specification focus provides you with the relevant description from the Edexcel specification, so that you can see exactly what the exam board expects you to know.

Support features help you to secure important knowledge, and **Stretch** features provide the opportunity for a challenge.

Sources of wisdom and authority will appear in boxes like this. Important, learnable phrases within a quote will often be in **bold**.

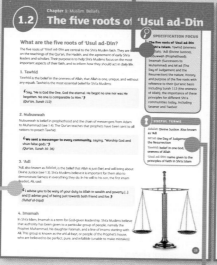

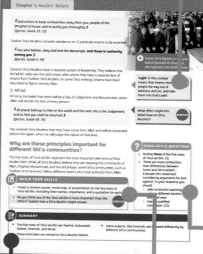

Exam-style questions gives two exam questions so that you can have a go at writing about the information you've studied in that topic. The letter at the start of each question tells you the question type (**a**, **b**, **c**, or **d**), and the number in brackets at the end tells you how many marks you are aiming for.

Useful terms are **orange** in the text and defined here. All of these useful terms are also provided in an alphabetical **glossary** at the end of the book.

Summary provides a short, bullet-pointed list of key information for ease of reference.

Build your skills are activities that focus on developing the skills you'll need for your exams, and consolidating the knowledge you'll need too.

- At the end of every chapter there are a few pages called 'Revision and Exam Practice'. These are designed to help you revise the information you have studied in that chapter, and coach you as you practise writing exam answers.

Four **exam-style questions** are provided – one for each of the question types **a**, **b**, **c**, and **d**.

Working through this Revision checklist, and following up on anything you might have missed, will help you to make sure you've revised all of the important information from the chapter.

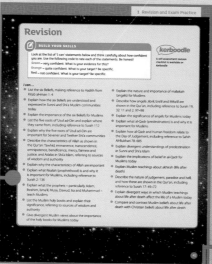

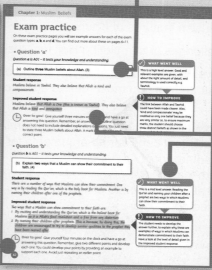

For each exam question, a sample **student answer** is provided, followed by an **improved** version so that you can be guided through improving your own answers.

What went well lists the good things about the first student response. **How to improve** lists its weaknesses, and suggests changes that should be made. These changes are reflected in the 'improved student response'.

Over to you! suggests that you have a go at answering the question yourself under exam conditions, and provides a few final exam tips.

Exam skills: What will the exams be like?

If you are studying the full course, you will sit **two** examinations, each **1 hour and 45 minutes** long. One exam will cover the content in this book (on Islam), and the other will cover a second faith option.

If you are studying the short course, you will sit **two** examinations, each **50 minutes** long. One exam will cover the first two chapters of content in this book (on Islam), and the other will cover a second faith option.

You must answer all of the questions on the exam paper.

Exam structure

Because this book covers just **one** of your two exams, the following information relates to that exam. For the full course exam, there will be **four questions** to answer. For the short course exam, there will be **two questions** to answer. Each question will relate to one of the four chapters in this book:

1. **Muslim Beliefs**

2. **Marriage and the Family**

Short course: answer two questions on these first two topics

3. **Living the Muslim Life**

4. **Matters of Life and Death**

Full course: answer four questions, one for each of these four topics

Each question will be split into four parts: **a**, **b**, **c**, **and d**. For example, your third question on the exam (covering *3. Living the Muslim Life*) could be something like this:

---

3 (a) Outline **three** Muslim features of Khums. (3)

(b) Explain **two** challenges of completing Hajj for Muslims. (4)

(c) Explain **two** ways that a Shi'a Muslim can show commitment to their faith. In your answer you must refer to a source of wisdom and authority. (5)

(d) "Salah is the most important of the Ten Obligatory Acts."
Evaluate this statement considering arguments for and against. In your response you should:
- refer to Muslim teachings
- refer to different Muslim points of view
- reach a justified conclusion. (15)

The 'a' question

The 'a' question will always start with the words 'Outline **three**…' or 'State **three**', and the maximum number of marks awarded will be three marks. For example:

> **3**   (a)   Outline **three** Muslim features of Khums.   **(3)**

The 'b' question

The 'b' question will always start with the words 'Explain **two**…' or 'Describe **two**…', and the maximum number of marks awarded will be four marks. For example:

>   (b)   Explain **two** challenges of completing Hajj for Muslims.   **(4)**

The 'c' question

The 'c' question will always start with the words 'Explain **two**…', and ask you to refer to a source of wisdom and authority. The maximum number of marks awarded will be five marks. For example:

>   (c)   Explain **two** ways that a Shi'a Muslim can show commitment to their faith. In your answer you must refer to a source of wisdom and authority.   **(5)**

The 'd' question

The 'd' question will always start with a statement of opinion that you are asked to evaluate. These questions will sometimes be out of 12 marks, and sometimes be out of 15 marks (see page 11, 'Written communication', to find out why). For example:

>   (d)   "Salah is the most important of the Ten Obligatory Acts."
> Evaluate this statement considering arguments for and against.
> In your response you should:
> * refer to Muslim teachings
> * refer to different Muslim points of view
> * reach a justified conclusion.   **(15)**

Know your question types!

…that way, nothing in your exam will take you by surprise!

Exam skills: How will the exams be marked?

When you're revising and practising using exam questions, it will really help you to understand how you'll be marked. If you know what the examiners are looking for, then you're more likely to do well!

Assessment Objectives

Examiners will mark your work using two Assessment Objectives: Assessment Objective 1 (AO1), and Assessment Objective 2 (AO2). The two Assessment Objectives are described in the table below.

	Students must	Weighting
AO1	Demonstrate knowledge and understanding of religion and belief, including: • beliefs, practices and sources of authority • influence on individuals, communities and societies • similarities and differences within and/or between religions and beliefs.	50%
AO2	Analyse and evaluate aspects of religion and belief, including their significance and influence.	50%

You need to remember that 50% of the marks available in your exam will be awarded for demonstrating **knowledge and understanding of religion and belief** (AO1), and 50% of the marks available will be awarded for **analysing and evaluating aspects of religion and belief** (AO2).

Marking the 'a' question

'Outline/State' questions are assessed using Assessment Objective 1 (knowledge) only. These questions require you to provide three facts or short ideas: **you don't need to explain them or express any opinions**. For example, in answer to the question 'Outline **three** Muslim features of Khums', your three responses could be:

1. Khums is paid by Shi'a Muslims. (1)

2. Shi'a Muslims give 20% of their savings every year to their leader. (1)

3. Khums is spent on orphanages, schools, mosques and other religious causes. (1)

For each response, you would receive 1 mark. You're not expected to spend time explaining lots of detail: the question only asks you to give three features.

Marking the 'b' question

Like the 'a' question, 'b' questions are assessed using Assessment Objective 1 (knowledge) only. However, 'b' questions start with 'Explain' or 'Describe', which means you will need to show **development** of ideas. For example, if the question is 'Explain **two** challenges of completing Hajj for Muslims' you might think you just need to state the two challenges, but this means you can only be awarded **a maximum of two marks**:

Challenge 1: It is physically demanding. (1)

Challenge 2: It is hard to maintain the lessons learned. (1)

The challenges given above are correct, but the student would only score 2 marks out of 4. In order to fully **explain** these reasons, you need to show some **development**. For example:

Type 1: It is physically demanding (1), **because there are lots of rituals to complete over about a five day period. (1)**

Type 2: It is hard to maintain the lessons learned (1), **because people return home to their daily lives after Hajj and it is challenging to remember the experience fully as a result. (1)**

Each of the above points are now developed, and would receive 2 marks each, totalling **4 marks**.

Marking the 'c' question

Like the 'a' and 'b' questions, 'c' questions are assessed using Assessment Objective 1 (knowledge) only. 'c' questions are very similar to 'b' questions (they begin with 'Explain two' and require two developed points), but they have one crucial difference. For an extra mark, you are expected to include a reference to a **source of wisdom and authority**, which could be a quotation from/reference to the Qur'an or another important source within Islam. For example, here's a student answer to a five mark question:

> (c) Explain **two** ways that a Shi'a Muslim can show commitment to their faith. In your answer you must refer to a source of wisdom and authority. **(5)**
>
> Shi'a Muslims can show commitment to their faith by setting aside time to pray to Allah **(1)**. This is called Salah, which is prescribed at set times and is one of the Ten Obligatory Acts **(1)**: 'prayer is obligatory for the believers at prescribed times' (Qur'an 4: 103) **(1)**.
>
> They can also show commitment by paying 20% of their savings to the Imam **(1)**. This is called Khums, and it is given to improve education and relieve poverty in the Muslim community **(1)**.

You need to write **two** developed points, one of which needs to be supported by a source of wisdom and authority. Setting out your writing in two paragraphs makes it clear that it is two developed points. You could directly quote a source, or you could just include the reference.

CONNECTIVES

A **connective** helps you to develop your basic answer. There are lots of different types of connective (therefore/because/and/consequently/a result of this is/this means that/this is). However, take care not to simply repeat the question and then use a connective, as that is not a developed answer and is only worth one mark. For example, 'There are two challenges of completing Hajj, **and** one of these is because it is physically demanding' would only receive one mark despite the use of a connective.

Marking the 'd' question

The 'd' questions are marked using AO2 (analysis/evaluation). These questions specifically ask you to evaluate a statement. Evaluating a statement means that you are weighing up how good or true it is. The best way to evaluate something is to consider different opinions on the matter – and this is exactly what the question asks you to do. When you are planning your answer, you need to remember to do the following:

- Refer to Muslim teachings – for instance core beliefs and important sources of wisdom and authority
- Ensure that different viewpoints are included either from within Islam or non-religious views, and ensure that relevant ethical theories are referred to (the question will make it clear which of these will be required in your answer)
- Ensure that you include a justified conclusion – in other words, your final decision on the matter having considered different viewpoints.

If you don't refer to different viewpoints, **you cannot get more than half of the marks**.

The examiner will mark your answer using a **mark scheme**, similar to the one below.

Level 1 (1–3 marks)	• Basic information or reasons about the issue are identified and can be explained by some religious or moral understanding. • Opinions are given but not fully explained.
Level 2 (4–6 marks)	• Some information or reasons about the issue are loosely identified and can be explained by limited religious or moral understanding. • Opinions are given which attempt to support the issue but are not fully explained or justified.
Level 3 (7–9 marks)	• Information given clearly describes religious information/issues, leading to coherent and logical chains of reasoning **that consider different viewpoints**. These are supported by an accurate understanding of religion and belief. • The answer contains coherent and reasoned judgements of many, but not all, of the elements in the question. Judgements are supported by a good understanding of evidence, leading to a partially justified conclusion.
Level 4 (10–12 marks)	• The response critically deconstructs religious information/issues, leading to coherent and logical chains of reasoning **that consider different viewpoints**. These are supported by a sustained, accurate and thorough understanding of religion and belief. • The answer contains coherent and reasoned judgements of the full range of elements in the question. Judgements are fully supported by the comprehensive use of evidence, leading to a fully justified conclusion.

ARE YOU READY?

Written communication

Some of the marks in your exam will be awarded purely for the quality of your 'written communication'. Written communication includes your use of correct **spelling, punctuation and grammar**, as well as the use of **specialist terminology**.

These marks will be awarded in questions **1(d)** and **3(d)**: These are the long essay questions on topics 1 and 3 (*Muslim Beliefs* and *Living the Muslim Life*). Whereas 'd' questions in topics 2 and 4 are out of 12 marks, these will be out of **15 marks**, and the extra 3 marks in each question are awarded solely for your written communication. You'll know which questions these are in the exam because they will be shown with an asterisk (*) and have a really clear instruction above them:

> **In this question, 3 of the marks awarded will be for your spelling, punctuation and grammar and your use of specialist terminology.**
>
> *(d) "Salah is the most important of the Ten Obligatory Acts."
> Evaluate this statement considering arguments for and against. In your response you should:
> * refer to Muslim teachings
> * refer to different Muslim points of view
> * reach a justified conclusion.
> (15)

In these questions:

* 0 marks are awarded if there are considerable errors or irrelevant information
* 1 mark is awarded for reasonable accuracy and limited use of religious terms
* 2 marks are awarded for considerable accuracy and a good number of specialist terms
* 3 marks are awarded for consistent accuracy and a wide range of specialist terms.

Good written communication is always important, but you will only receive marks for it in questions **1(d)** and **3(d)**. Therefore, you should allow yourself time in your exam to check these two essays carefully and amend any errors.

Introduction to Islam

What is Islam?

Islam is the second largest religious tradition within Great Britain today. Other faiths include Christianity, Buddhism, Hinduism, Judaism and Sikhism. Christianity is the main religious tradition of Great Britain.

Islam is the name of the religion that Muslims follow. The word 'Islam' is Arabic and has a number of meanings, including 'peace', 'submission' and 'obedience'. Islam was taught in a series of messages and laws given by Allah (God) (see 1.3) to human beings through special people called prophets and messengers (see 1.4) over many centuries in different parts of the world. The final law was given to the Prophet Muhammad in Arabia in the 7th century.

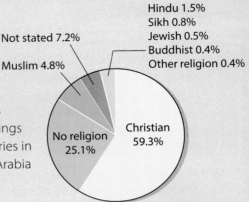

Hindu 1.5%
Sikh 0.8%
Jewish 0.5%
Buddhist 0.4%
Other religion 0.4%

Not stated 7.2%

Muslim 4.8%

No religion 25.1%

Christian 59.3%

The 2011 England and Wales census asked people, 'What is your religion?'. This pie chart shows how people responded

What do Muslims believe?

The word 'Muslim' means someone who submits to Allah. Every Muslim has to affirm a core belief called the Shahadah, which means believing in Allah and in Muhammad as His Messenger (see 3.2). Collectively, Muslims belong to the ummah (global Islamic community).

Muslims believe Islam is a universal religion, for all people and all times. Muslim beliefs are summarized in the six Beliefs (Chapter 1) and the Five Pillars (3.2–3.6). Messages that Allah gave to humans are contained in holy books and other texts (sources of wisdom and authority). The most important of these is the Qur'an (1.5).

Muslims learn their religion through three main sources:

1. Qur'an – this is the final and perfect scripture, revealed by Allah to the Prophet Muhammad through the angel Jibril (1.6)

2. Sunnah – this is the practice of the Prophet Muhammad, including things that he did (for example, eat and drink) and the way he did them (for example, with his right hand while sitting down)

3. Hadith – these are the words of the Prophet Muhammad, including teachings and guidance which are not included in the Qur'an.

These form the basis of the shari'ah (Islamic legal system), which Muslims must follow. Muslims will also consult scholars and leaders in their communities for a better understanding about their religion. These figures play an important role in Muslim communities as they offer advice and guidance on how to practice Islam and live as Muslims.

What are the different groups within Islam?

As with followers in other religions, Muslims are very diverse – there are several schools of thought in Islam, which means that many Muslims understand and interpret some beliefs and teachings differently.

The two main branches in Islam are called Sunni and Shi'a, which you will be learning more about in this book. Sunni Muslims make up approximately 85% of the ummah, and Shi'a Muslims around 15%. There are many groups and sects within as well as outside Sunni and Shi'a that are represented in Great Britain. These include Deobandi, Barelwi, Salafi, Ithna 'Ashari (Twelver Shi'a), Ahmadiyya, Isma'ili and Sufi. The place of some groups in Islam is questioned, by others. Some differences are significant and are due to divergent attitudes on a range of issues. Ahmadiyya Muslims, for example, believe in Mirza Ghulam Ahmad (died 1908) as the Messiah and Mahdi (guided leader) promised in Islam, and that he was a Muslim prophet who came to revive its original teachings. Other Muslims do not accept Ahmad's prophethood, and for this reason many of them do not consider Ahmadiyya Muslims as part of Islam. However, Ahmadiyya Muslims still identify themselves as Muslims as they say they believe in the Qur'an, the Sunnah, and the Hadith. Other groups in Islam hold differing views ranging from whether women can lead men in prayer to the permissibility of celebrating the Prophet Muhammad's birthday (Mawlid al-Nabi). Many Barelwi Muslims, for instance, celebrate Mawlid al-Nabi, while other Muslims do not.

Islam in Great Britain today

There are three million Muslims in Great Britain today. Muslims pray in mosques, which are houses dedicated to the worship of God (see 3.3). They can be identified by their architecture and certain features, like a dome and minaret. Most mosques in Great Britain belong to a particular denomination.

Often we see Islam dominate the headlines because a number of extremist acts are committed by people claiming to be Muslims. This can lead people to associate the religion with violence. The vast majority of Muslims reject terrorism, and say that a proper study of Islam can lead to a greater understanding of its true values. This book provides you with opportunities to make your own observations, raise questions and draw personal conclusions about various teachings, beliefs and important issues.

B The Ismaili Centre, London

A Birmingham Central Mosque

C Noor Mosque, Crawley

D Imam Khoei Islamic Centre, London

Chapter 1:
Muslim Beliefs

Chapter contents	Specification mapping	Page
Chapter 1: Muslim Beliefs	Section 1: Muslim Beliefs	14
1.1 The six Beliefs	1.1 The six Beliefs of Islam: their nature, history and purpose including Kitab al-iman 1:4; how they are understood and expressed in Sunni and Shi'a Muslim communities today; the importance of these principles for Muslims	16
1.2 The five roots of 'Usul ad-Din	1.2 The five roots of 'Usul ad-Din in Shi'a Islam Tawhid (oneness of Allah); 'Adl (Divine Justice); Nubuwwah (Prophethood); Imamah (Successors to Muhammad) and Mi'ad (The Day of Judgement and the Resurrection): the nature, history and purpose of the five roots with reference to their Qur'anic basis including Surah 112 (the oneness of Allah); the importance of these principles for different Shi'a communities today, including Sevener and Twelver	19
1.3 The nature of Allah	1.3 The nature of Allah: how the characteristics of Allah are shown in the Qur'an and why they are important: Tawhid (oneness), including Surah 16: 35–36, immanence, transcendence, omnipotence, beneficence, mercy, fairness and justice, Adalat in Shi'a Islam	21
1.4 Risalah	1.4 Risalah: the nature and importance of prophethood for Muslims, including Surah 2: 136; what the roles of prophets teach Muslims, exemplified in the lives of Adam, Ibrahim, Isma'il, Musa, Dawud, Isa, Muhammad	24
1.5 Muslim holy books	1.5 Muslim holy books (kutub): the nature, history, significance and purpose of Muslim holy books with reference to the Qur'an including Surah 53: 4–18, Tawrat (Torah) including Surah 5: 43–48, Zabur (Psalms) including Surah 4: 163–171, Injil (Gospel) including Surah 5: 46, Sahifah (Scrolls); divergent Muslim views about the importance of the holy books in their lives today	28
1.6 Malaikah	1.6 Malaikah: the nature and importance of angels for Muslims; how angels Jibril, Izra'il and Mika'il are shown in the Qur'an, including Surah 19, 32: 11 and 2: 97–98, and their significance for Muslims today	31
1.7 Al-Qadr	1.7 Al-Qadr: the nature and importance of predestination for Muslims; how al-Qadr and human freedom relates to the Day of Judgement, including reference to Sahih Al-Bukhari 78: 685; divergent understandings of predestination in Sunni and Shi'a Islam; the implications of belief in al-Qadr for Muslims today	34
1.8 Akhirah *This topic should be compared with Christianity.*	1.8 Akhirah: Muslim teachings about life after death; the nature of judgement, paradise and hell; how they are shown in the Qur'an, including Surah 17: 49–72; divergent ways in which Muslim teachings about life after death affect the life of a Muslim today	37
Revision and Exam Practice	**Revision checklist, exam questions, sample answers and guidance**	41

1.1 The six Beliefs

The six Beliefs of Islam: their nature, history and purpose including Kitab al-iman 1: 4; how they are understood and expressed in Sunni and Shi'a Muslim communities today; the importance of these principles for Muslims

There are many beliefs and teachings in Islam. While all Muslims hold very similar beliefs, they also have some differences. This often depends on what denomination (religious group) they may belong to. There are two main groups in Islam: **Sunni** and **Shi'a**.

Why did the Sunni and Shi'a Muslim split occur?

Following the death of the Prophet Muhammad, the founder of Islam, there was disagreement over who should have led the Muslim community. Sunni Muslims accepted the authority of Abu Bakr, who was known as the first rightly guided **khalifah**, while Shi'a Muslims felt Ali should have been the leader. Shi'a Muslims say all leaders should be from the **ahl al-bayt**, such as Ali because he was raised in Muhammad's house.

This disagreement led to the community splitting and the two groups developing their own understanding of Islam. The six Beliefs are central to the faith of all Muslims. Shi'a Muslims also follow the five roots of 'Usul ad-Din (see 1.2).

Ahl al-bayt: people of the Prophet Muhammad's house (family)

Allah: Arabic name for God

Hadith: sayings of the Prophet Muhammad

Khalifah: a religious leader (caliph), representing Allah or a prophet

Kitab al-iman: the Book of Faith in the Sahih Muslim collection of Hadith

Qur'an: the holiest text in Islam

Shi'a: Muslims who believe that leadership belongs to the ahl al-bayt

Sunni: Muslims who believe Abu Bakr was the first of four 'rightly guided' leaders after the Prophet Muhammad

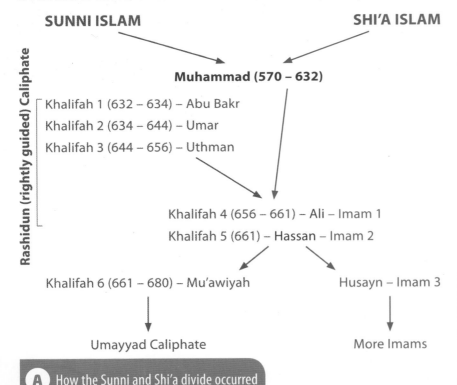

SUNNI ISLAM **SHI'A ISLAM**

Muhammad (570 – 632)

Rashidun (rightly guided) Caliphate

Khalifah 1 (632 – 634) – Abu Bakr
Khalifah 2 (634 – 644) – Umar
Khalifah 3 (644 – 656) – Uthman

Khalifah 4 (656 – 661) – Ali – Imam 1
Khalifah 5 (661) – Hassan – Imam 2

Khalifah 6 (661 – 680) – Mu'awiyah   Husayn – Imam 3

Umayyad Caliphate   More Imams

A How the Sunni and Shi'a divide occurred

What are the six Beliefs?

Sunni Muslims base their six central Beliefs, known as Iman al-Mufassal, on the **Qur'an** and the '**Hadith** of Gabriel', reported by 'Umar, a prominent follower of the Prophet Muhammad:

'Hadith' are a collection of sayings of the Prophet Muhammad. There are many compilations of Hadith. For Sunni Muslims, the most reliable books of Hadith are known as Al Sihah Al Sittah ('The Authentic Six', such as Sahih Al-Bukhari and Sahih Muslim). For Shi'a Muslims, the most popular sources of Hadith are called Al Kutub Al Arb'ah ('The Four Books', including Al Kafi and Man la yahduruhu al-Faqih). The Hadith of Gabriel is taken from Sahih Muslim and is found in Kitab al-iman ('Book of Faith').

SUPPORT

❛While we were one day sitting with the Messenger of Allah, there appeared before us a man dressed in extremely white clothes and with very black hair. No traces of travel were visible on him, and none of us knew him. He sat down close by the Prophet [... and] he went on to say, "Inform me about faith". The Messenger of Allah answered, "It is that you **believe in Allah, and His angels, and His books, and His messengers, and in the Last Day, and in the decree of Allah**" [... Later] the man went off. I waited a while, and then the Messenger of Allah said, "Umar, do you know who that questioner was? [...] That was Gabriel. He came to teach you your religion."❜
(Hadith – Sahih Muslim, Kitab al-iman 1: 1–4)

> **'Messenger of Allah'** is a phrase used to describe the Prophet Muhammad. In this story, a man called Umar is sitting with Muhammad, when they are approached by the angel Gabriel (Jibril). What does Gabriel ask the Prophet, and what answer does he get?
>
> **SUPPORT**

The six Beliefs are specified in this Hadith:

1. **Belief in Allah**: this is the most important belief for Muslims. **Allah** is the Supreme Being, creator of the universe. Without him, nothing would exist (see 1.3).

2. **Belief in the angels of Allah**: angels (called 'malaikah' in Arabic) are heavenly beings created by Allah to perform various tasks, such as delivering his messages to people (see 1.6).

3. **Belief in the books of Allah**: Muslims believe that Allah's messages are contained in holy texts known as kutubullah, or books of Allah. These include the Sahifah (Scrolls), Tawrat (Torah), Zabur (Psalms), Injil (Gospels), and finally the Qur'an (see 1.5).

4. **Belief in the messengers of Allah**: a messenger, or prophet, is a person chosen by Allah to teach and guide people to the right path. Muslims believe more than 124,000 prophets have appeared in the world and that it is essential to believe in all of them (see 1.4).

5. **Belief in the Day of Judgement**: the Qur'an teaches that eventually the entire universe will end. The dead will be resurrected and accounts will be taken of their deeds. Allah will judge whether people go to jannah (paradise) or jahannam (hell) (see 1.8).

6. **Belief in the decree of Allah**: Muslims believe in al-Qadr (divine decree) (see 1.7), also known as taqdir. Muslims believe that Allah has supreme power over the universe. He has also given humans free will, making us responsible for our own destiny. Allah will not interfere unless he wishes to.

The Beliefs highlight the key features of a Muslim's faith in Islam, and inform their day-to-day living.

How are the six Beliefs understood and expressed in Muslim communities today?

Muslims believe the six Beliefs should always be reflected in their actions and behaviour.

- Recognizing Allah as the creator encourages Muslims to be thankful for the life they have been given, and to express gratitude through prayer.

- Muslims are taught to respect the malaikah of Allah. When Muslims end their prayers they turn their heads to the right and left and say, 'peace be upon you' to the angels and anyone else they are praying next to.

- Many Muslims study the kutubullah as a way to improve their knowledge about different religious teachings. Lessons on other religious texts are also taught in some mosques to help Muslims develop their understanding about different faiths.

- Muslims are taught about, and many named after, different prophets so that they can learn from their example.

- Belief in the Day of Judgement reminds Muslims about their limited time on earth and the inevitable meeting with Allah, as expressed at funerals when a Muslim community comes together.

- Al-Qadr teaches Muslims about the need to accept God's will, and many Muslims seek blessings on a special night called Laylat al-Qadr, or 'Night of Power' (see 3.4).

B Muslim community at a funeral in the UK

Why are these principles important for Muslims?

The six Beliefs, mentioned in the **Kitab al-iman** Hadith, form the foundation of Sunni Muslims' faith. It is compulsory to believe in each of the principles. By following these beliefs, Sunni Muslims believe they are on the right path and will earn the pleasure of Allah.

BUILD YOUR SKILLS

1 Copy and complete the following table. The first row has been completed for you, to help you:

The six Beliefs	What do they mean?	How are they expressed in the Muslim community today
Belief in Allah	The most important belief is in the supreme being Allah. He created the universe and, without him, nothing would exist.	This belief encourages Muslims to be grateful for all Allah has done. They express this gratitude through prayer and worship.

2 Is it important for beliefs to be expressed with others in the community? Explain your answer.

3 'Belief in the Day of Judgement is the most important belief in Islam.' Do you agree with this statement? Explain your views. **STRETCH**

SUMMARY

- There are two main groups within Islam: Sunni and Shi'a Muslims.
- Sunni Muslims believe in the six Beliefs, known as Iman al-Mufassal. Shi'a Muslims also accept these.
- The principles outlined in these beliefs are the foundations of Sunni Muslims' faith and inform their day-to-day living.

EXAM-STYLE QUESTIONS

a State **three** religious traditions other than Islam in Great Britain today. (3)

b Explain **two** reasons why the six Beliefs are important to Muslims. (4)

Chapter 1: Muslim Beliefs
The five roots of 'Usul ad-Din

What are the five roots of 'Usul ad-Din?

The five roots of **'Usul ad-Din** are central to the Shi'a Muslim faith. They are based on the teachings of the Qur'an, the Hadith, and the agreement of early Shi'a leaders and scholars. Their purpose is to help Shi'a Muslims focus on the most important aspects of their faith, and to inform how they should act in daily life.

1. Tawhid

Tawhid is the belief in the oneness of Allah, that Allah is one, unique, and without any equals. Tawhid is the most essential belief for Shi'a Muslims:

> ❝Say, "He is God the One, God the eternal. He begot no one nor was He begotten. No one is comparable to Him."❞
> *(Qur'an, Surah 112)*

2. Nubuwwah

Nubuwwah is belief in prophethood and the chain of messengers from Adam to Muhammad (see 1.4). The Qur'an teaches that prophets have been sent to all nations to preach Tawhid:

> ❝**We sent a messenger to every community**, saying, "Worship God and shun false gods."❞
> *(Qur'an, Surah 16: 36)*

3. 'Adl

'Adl, also known as **Adalat**, is the belief that Allah is just (fair) and will bring about Divine Justice (see 1.3). Shi'a Muslims believe it is important for them also to demonstrate fairness in everything they do. In his will to his son, the first imam (leader), Ali, said:

> ❝I advise you to be wary of your duty to Allah in wealth and poverty [...] and [I advise you] of being just towards both friend and foe.❞
> *(Tuhaf al-Uqul)*

4. Imamah

In Shi'a Islam, Imamah is a term for God-given leadership. Shi'a Muslims believe that authority has been given to a particular group of people, namely the Prophet Muhammad, his daughter Fatimah, and a line of imams starting with Ali. This group is known as the ahl al-bayt, or people of the Prophet's house, who are believed to be perfect, pure, and infallible (unable to make mistakes):

USEFUL TERMS

Adalat: Divine Justice. Also known as 'Adl

Mi'ad: the Day of Judgement and the Resurrection

Tawhid: belief in one God; the oneness of Allah

'Usul ad-Din: name given to the principles of faith in Shi'a Islam

> ❛God wishes to keep uncleanness away from you, people of the [Prophet's] House, and to purify you thoroughly. ❜
> *(Qur'an, Surah 33: 33)*

Twelver Shi'a Muslims consider obedience to 12 particular imams to be essential:

> ❛You who believe, obey God and the Messenger, **and those in authority among you**. ❜
> *(Qur'an, Surah 4: 59)*

A Twelver Shi'a Muslims in Iran pray behind Ayatollah Ali Khamenei, who represents the twelfth Imam

Sevener Shi'a Muslims have a separate system of leadership. They believe that Ism'ail ibn Jafar was the sixth imam, after whom they have a separate line of imams from Twelver Shi'a Muslims. In some Shi'a writings, imams have been described as 'lights' sent by Allah.

5. Mi'ad

Mi'ad is the belief that there will be a Day of Judgement and Resurrection, when Allah will decide the fate of every person:

> ❛all praise belongs to Him in this world and the next; His is the Judgement; and to Him you shall be returned. ❜
> *(Qur'an, Surah 28: 70)*

'Light' in this context means that imams show people the way out of darkness and sin, and take them into God's path. — **SUPPORT**

What effect might this belief have on Shi'a Muslims? — **STRETCH**

This reminds Shi'a Muslims that they have come from Allah and will be presented before him again, when he will judge the nature of their lives.

Why are these principles important for different Shi'a communities?

The five roots of 'Usul ad-Din represent the most important elements of Shi'a Muslim faith. While all Shi'a Muslims believe they are obeying the commands of Allah, Prophet Muhammad, and the ahl al-bayt, some Shi'a communities, such as Twelvers and Seveners, follow different imams who have authority from Allah.

BUILD YOUR SKILLS

1 Create a revision poster, mind-map, or presentation on the five roots of 'Usul ad-Din, including their names, importance, and a quotation for each.

2 Do you think one of the 'Usul ad-Din is more important than the others? Explain how a Shi'a Muslim might answer. — **STRETCH**

 EXAM-STYLE QUESTIONS

a Outline **three** of the five roots of 'Usul ad-Din. (3)

d 'There are more similarities than differences between Sunni and Shi'a beliefs.' Evaluate this statement considering arguments for and against. In your response you should:
   • refer to Muslim teachings
   • refer to different Muslim points of view
   • reach a justified conclusion. (15)

SUMMARY

• The five roots of 'Usul ad-Din are Tawhid, Nubuwwah, Adalat, Imamah, and Mi'ad.

• These principles are central to Shi'a Muslim beliefs.

• Some aspects, like Imamah, are followed differently by different Shi'a communities.

1.3 The nature of Allah

The Arabic word for God is 'Allah'. Muslims believe it is impossible to visualize Allah because he is not a physical being. In Islam, any attempt to draw him is forbidden.

How are the characteristics of Allah shown in the Qur'an?

Muslims believe that Allah has many characteristics. More than 100 characteristics of Allah appear in the Qur'an and the Hadith.

Compassionate
Friend
Lord of all beings
Protector
Creator

All-seeing
Merciful
Everlasting

A Some characteristics of Allah. The calligraphy shows 'Allah' in Arabic

SPECIFICATION FOCUS

The nature of Allah: how the characteristics of Allah are shown in the Qur'an and why they are important: Tawhid (oneness), including Surah 16: 35–36, immanence, transcendence, omnipotence, beneficence, mercy, fairness and justice, Adalat in Shi'a Islam

USEFUL TERMS

Beneficence: kindness, generosity

Immanence: a belief that Allah acts in the world

Omnipotence: being all-powerful

Sin: an action against Allah's will

Surah: chapter

Transcendence: a belief that Allah is above and beyond his creation

How can Allah have so many characteristics and still be one being? Muslims believe that just as human beings can be kind, fair, and a friend, so can Allah – but even more so. Muslims believe humans cannot fully understand his nature.

The following are just some of the characteristics of Allah.

Tawhid

Tawhid means 'oneness' and is the belief that Allah is unique and without any partner (see 1.2), including parents, siblings, or children:

> ❛ Are the messengers obliged to do anything other than deliver [their message] clearly? We sent a messenger to every community, saying, **"Worship God and shun false gods."** ❜
> (Qur'an, Surah 16: 35–36)

To associate partners with Allah, including 'false gods', is shirk – the worst **sin** in Islam.

Immanence and transcendence

Muslims believe that Allah is the creator of everything. They believe there are parts of his creation that humans can observe and experience, but that much of it is beyond human understanding. Muslims have a similar understanding of Allah, that he is both **immanent** and is **transcendent**.

The Qur'an contains many examples of Allah's immanence and how he sustains the universe. It also describes how close he is to humans and, through the actions of angels, records everything that happens.

> ❝We shall certainly question those to whom messengers were sent [...] for **We were never far from them**, We shall tell them what they did.❞
> *(Qur'an, Surah 7: 6–7)*

> ❝We created man – We know what his soul whispers to him: **We are closer to him than his jugular vein.**❞
> *(Qur'an, Surah 50: 16)*

Allah's transcendence is also described in the Qur'an:

> ❝Your Lord is God, who created the heavens and earth in six Days, then **established Himself on the throne** [...] all creation and command belong to Him. **Exalted be God**, Lord of all the worlds!❞
> *(Qur'an, Surah 7: 54)*

In this verse, the Qur'an refers to Allah seating himself 'on the throne', which many Muslims understand as symbolic of his control over everything.

Omnipotence

Muslims believe Allah has the power to create everything from nothing, and is able to do whatever he wills. He is **omnipotent**, the only authority in the universe:

> ❝Do you not know that control of the heavens and the earth belongs to Him? You [believers] have no protector or helper but God [...] **He has power over all things.**❞
> *(Qur'an, Surah 2: 107–109)*

Beneficence

Muslims believe Allah is the most **beneficent** of all beings and that he loves his creation, especially humans. His kindness knows no limits:

> ❝your Lord's bounty is not restricted.❞
> *(Qur'an, Surah 17: 20)*

Mercy

There are 114 chapters in the Qur'an. A chapter is known as a **surah**. Each of them (apart from Surah 9) starts with the words: 'In the name of God, the Lord of Mercy, the Giver of Mercy'. The Qur'an also says:

> ❝My mercy embraces all things.❞
> *(Qur'an, Surah 7: 156)*

SUPPORT
The jugular vein is one of several major blood vessels in the human neck. This verse shows how close Allah is to every person.

STRETCH
'Exalted' is another word for transcendent – it means to be high up. Use two sentences to explain the difference between immanence and transcendence.

B The 'throne' in the Qur'an is a metaphor for Allah's omnipotence

SUPPORT
To **'give mercy'** means to show kindness to someone when you could otherwise punish them. Why do you think this characteristic is mentioned at the start of each surah?

These verses show the importance of Allah's benevolent nature. Muslims believe that everything Allah does is as an act of kindness, including punishment (which acts like medicine to heal the infected part of the soul). Many Muslims believe that hell is not forever, so even those who are punished will enter paradise once they have been purified of their sins.

Fairness and justice, Adalat in Shi'a Islam

Both Sunni and Shi'a Muslims believe that Allah is just. For Shi'a Muslims, Adalat (Divine Justice) is one of the five roots of 'Usul ad-Din (see 1.2). Being just means that Allah treats people fairly according to how they have lived their life.

This aspect of Allah's nature teaches Muslims that they are accountable for what they have and have not done. Allah expects people to show fairness in everything they do:

> ❝ God commands you [people] to return things entrusted to you to their rightful owners, and, **if you judge between people, to do so with justice**: God's instructions to you are excellent, for He hears and sees everything. ❞
> *(Qur'an, Surah 4: 58)*

Why are these characteristics important?

- While Muslims believe it is impossible to fully comprehend Allah, knowing some of his attributes helps them to understand something of his nature.

- Understanding Allah's nature enables Muslims to establish a close relationship with him through worship, which, according to the Qur'an, is the very reason why humans were created (Surah 51: 56).

- Knowing about Allah can also help Muslims strive to reflect certain divine attributes. For instance, if Allah is beneficent, then they should aim to be the same and show this through their actions. That way, humans can become a reflection of some of Allah's characteristics (Surah 2: 138).

STRETCH Is it possible to believe in a God who is compassionate but also punishes? What would an atheist say, and why? And how might a Muslim respond?

C Muslims recite many of the names of Allah during prayer

BUILD YOUR SKILLS

1 Create a revision mind-map. On your mind-map, include:
   a the meaning of Tawhid, immanence, transcendence, omnipotence, beneficence, mercy, fairness, and justice (Adalat)
   b a short, memorable quotation from the Qur'an for each characteristic
   c an explanation for why each characteristic is important.

2 Do you think it is possible to believe in a God that cannot be understood fully? Explain your reasons.

EXAM-STYLE QUESTIONS

b Explain **two** reasons why the characteristics of Allah are important for Muslims. (4)
c Explain **two** Muslim beliefs about Allah. In your answer you must refer to a source of wisdom and authority. (5)

SUMMARY

- Muslims believe that Allah has many characteristics, including Tawhid, immanence, transcendence, omnipotence, beneficence, mercy, fairness, and justice (Adalat).

- The names of Allah tell Muslims something about his nature, but it is impossible to understand him fully.

- Allah's characteristics are important because they can help Muslims to worship and aspire to be a reflection of him.

1.4 Risalah

What is the nature of prophethood for Muslims?

Muslims believe Allah is a personal God who can be communicated with directly. They also believe that special individuals are chosen by Allah to teach **humanity** about the right way to live. These people are called **prophets**.

Belief in **Risalah**, also known as Nubuwwah, is important to Muslims for several reasons:

- It is one of the six Beliefs for Sunnis and the five roots of 'Usul ad-Din for Shi'as.
- It represents how Allah communicates to people.
- Allah has spoken to many prophets, and Muslims are required to follow their teachings.
- All the prophets demonstrated great qualities and set an example of how to live. Many Muslims name their children after prophets and strive to raise them to imitate them.
- It reminds Muslims of the common heritage they share with other faiths, particularly Judaism and Christianity.

The Prophet Muhammad said that more than 124,000 prophets have appeared in different parts of the world, and it is essential for Muslims to believe in all of them.

> ❛every community has been sent a warner [prophet].❜
> *(Qur'an, Surah 35: 24)*

Adam, Ibrahim, Isma'il, Musa, Dawud, Isa, and Muhammad are examples of prominent prophets.

> ❛So [you believers], say, "We believe in God and in what was sent down to us and what was sent down to Abraham, Ishmael, Isaac, Jacob, and the Tribes, and what was given to Moses, Jesus, and all the prophets by their Lord. We make no distinction between any of them..."❜
> *(Qur'an, Surah 2: 136)*

What do the roles of prophets teach Muslims?

Muslims believe that the roles of prophets are highly significant as they live exemplary lives, setting good examples of individual, social, moral and spiritual conduct, and communicating the message of God to others. Muslims use the Qur'an, the Hadith, and other texts to know more about particular messengers and what messages they brought to humanity.

Adam

Adam is believed to be the first prophet. He has been called Allah's khalifah (representative), whom the angels had to serve.

SPECIFICATION FOCUS

Risalah: the nature and importance of prophethood for Muslims, including Surah 2: 136; what the roles of prophets teach Muslims, exemplified in the lives of Adam, Ibrahim, Isma'il, Musa, Dawud, Isa, Muhammad

USEFUL TERMS

Humanity: all human beings

Miracles: extraordinary events that may not be explainable

Prophet: a messenger chosen by Allah to teach humanity what is right and wrong

Risalah: the system of communication between Allah and people, through prophets

Scripture: a holy book or text given by Allah through a prophet

Adam is regarded highly in the Qur'an because he was chosen by Allah over all the people of his time (Surah 3: 33) and Allah treated him with great mercy.

Adam and Hawwa (Eve) lived in a beautiful garden and were told to enjoy its comforts. They were also commanded to keep away from a 'tree' which represented evil, but they were deceived – 'Satan made them slip' (Surah 2: 36). This resulted in them both being banished from the garden. However, Muslims believe it is impossible for a prophet to commit any sin and that approaching the symbolic tree was simply a mistake.

The story of Adam teaches Muslims to follow Allah's commands and not to allow Satan (the devil) to tempt them.

Ibrahim

Ibrahim (Abraham) is considered by Muslims to be one of the greatest prophets. He is called Allah's 'friend' (Surah 4: 125) and was also one of the Prophet Muhammad's ancestors.

> ❝ Abraham [Ibrahim] was truly an example: devoutly obedient to God and true in faith [...] **he was thankful for the blessings of God who chose him and guided him to a straight path**. We gave him blessings in this world, and he is among the righteous in the Hereafter. ❞
> *(Qur'an, Surah 16: 120–122)*

These verses show the high status of Ibrahim. He was an 'example' to others, 'obedient' to God, and highly honoured in both this world and the afterlife. Ibrahim was extremely committed to his faith and family, and wanted his children to serve Allah too.

The account of Ibrahim shows Muslims the high moral standards he reached and the importance of learning from his life and faith.

A The Ka'bah was rebuilt by Ibrahim and Isma'il

It was Ibrahim's prayer for a prophet to be born in the future that Muslims believe was fulfilled by the appearance of Muhammad.

> ❝ "[...] Our Lord, **make a messenger of their own rise up from among them**, to recite Your revelations to them, teach them the Scripture and wisdom, and purify them [...]" ❞
> *(Qur'an, Surah 2: 129)*

SUPPORT

The Ka'bah is a cube-shaped building in Makkah which Muslims believe was the first house of Allah on earth, and is where the annual Hajj pilgrimage (see 3.6) takes place.

Isma'il

Isma'il (Ishmael), one of Ibrahim's sons, was also a prophet. Muslims believe Ibrahim and Isma'il were chosen to rebuild the Ka'bah in Makkah.

The Qur'an (Surah 37: 100–111) relates how Ibrahim had seen a dream from Allah that he was sacrificing Isma'il. When he shared this with his son, Isma'il did not hesitate to offer his life. Just as Ibrahim was about to sacrifice Isma'il, God called out to him to stop and praised them both for their spirit of dedication.

Through this story, Muslims are taught to always trust and put Allah first, and to be prepared to offer themselves for the service of faith. This event is commemorated at Id-ul-Adha (see 3.8).

Musa

Musa (Moses) was the main founder of Judaism. Muslims believe that Musa was appointed by Allah to free the Banu Isra'il (Israelites) from slavery under the harsh rule of Fir'awn (Pharaoh) in Egypt. He was given the Al-Kitab (**scripture**) and Al-Furqan (the ability to distinguish right and wrong):

> ‘ We inscribed everything for him in the Tablets which taught and explained everything, saying, "Hold on to them firmly and urge your people to hold fast to their excellent teachings." ’
> *(Qur'an, Surah 7: 145)*

The prophethood of Musa is famous for many **miracles**, particularly the parting of the seas which allowed Musa and the Israelites to escape before the waters closed in to drown Fir'awn and his people who pursued them (Surah 26: 52–68).

For Muslims, Musa's life is an example of how Allah rewards perseverance in the face of suffering, and how good will overcome evil.

B The Tablets are better known as the Ten Commandments, which Muslims believe were given to Musa on Mount Sinai

Dawud

Dawud (David) was one of the messengers (rasuls) of the Banu Isra'il. He is remembered for his wisdom, prayers, and fasting, as well as for his victory against the oppressive Jalut (Goliath), after which he was made king of the Israelites:

> ‘ David killed Goliath, and God gave him sovereignty and wisdom and taught him what He pleased. ’
> *(Qur'an, Surah 2: 251)*

The Qur'an uses four titles for people appointed by Allah: rasul (messenger), nabi (prophet), nadhir (warner), and khalifah (representative). **SUPPORT**

This account confirms for Muslims that Allah gives honour to his chosen ones, and that they can be blessed with both worldly and spiritual honour.

Prayers by Musa and Dawud have been preserved in Islam and are regularly recited by Muslims.

Isa

Muslims believe Isa (Jesus) is among the most honoured prophets of Allah. The Injil, which was one of the most important revelations before the Qur'an, was revealed to Isa (see 1.5).

Isa's many miracles are described in the Qur'an, including his own birth, which did not involve a biological father. He is also attributed with creating birds out of clay and bringing the dead back to life (Surah 3: 49), although many Muslims understand these accounts to have a symbolic meaning (he brought people out of the darkness and into the light). The Qur'an rejects the Christian idea that Isa was divine and was killed on a cross. It states instead that Allah saved him (Surah 4: 157–158).

Muslims are taught about Isa being a prophet who honoured Tawhid (see 1.3). Muslims follow his example and worship Allah as one God.

 Muhammad was given the Qur'an

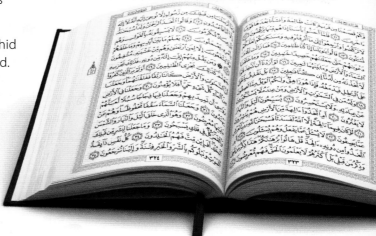

Muhammad

Muhammad is the principal prophet sent by Allah. Muslims believe he was the only prophet to have been given a universal message that was meant for all times, and that the previous prophets prepared the way for Muhammad. He is described as 'the seal of the prophets' (Surah 33: 40), meaning that the qualities of all the messengers were found in him. It also means that he was the last messenger to bring a revealed scripture: the Qur'an (see 1.5).

The Qur'an describes Muhammad as 'a light' (Surah 5: 15), a teacher of wisdom (Surah 62: 2), 'a mercy [...] to all people' (Surah 21: 107), and 'an excellent model' (Surah 33: 21). It also tells Muslims to offer prayers for him because of his honoured status:

> ❝ God and His angels bless the Prophet so, you who believe, **bless him too and give him greetings of peace**. ❞
> *(Qur'an, Surah 33: 56)*

The Qur'an teaches Muslims that they have been given the final guidance for humanity and that by following the example of Muhammad they will please Allah.

 BUILD YOUR SKILLS

1. Create a job description for a prophet. Decide what their responsibilities will be, and then identify the qualities and skills they need to complete them.

2. Write down at least three things that Muslims learn from the lives of prophets.

3. 'If Allah loves everyone equally, why does he choose special messengers?'
   a. How would a Muslim answer this question?
   b. How would a non-religious person answer this question?

 SUMMARY

- Risalah refers to the means of communication between Allah and people, through many thousands of prophets.

- Messengers (rasuls) are given the task of passing on Allah's guidance to humanity.

- Adam, Ibrahim, Isma'il, Musa, Dawud, Isa, and Muhammad are some of the prophets mentioned in the Qur'an.

? EXAM-STYLE QUESTIONS

a. Outline **three** things that Muslims believe about Risalah. (3)

b. Explain **two** reasons why Muhammad is an important prophet in Islam. (4)

1.5 Muslim holy books

What are the Muslim holy books and why are they significant?

Muslims believe that, over the centuries, prophets have received messages from Allah (see 1.4). Many of these messages were recorded in ancient scriptures (known as **kutubullah**), many of which have survived and continue to be a source of guidance for billions of people today.

Holy books revealed to humanity prior to the Qur'an are believed by Muslims to be earlier forms of **revelation** and, therefore, are not considered a final authority. However, they are still highly respected by Muslims.

Here are the books in chronological order.

Sahifah (Scrolls)

One of the earliest known texts is the **Sahifah** of Ibrahim and Moses. These 'scrolls' are believed to be lost and little is known about them. However, some parts of the Sahifah have been preserved, as they are quoted in the Qur'an. These verses give Muslims an indication of what was taught in the Sahifah:

> ❛ Has he not been told **what was written in the Scriptures of Moses [Musa] and of Abraham [Ibrahim]** [...] that no soul shall bear the burden of another; that man will only have what he has worked towards [...] that the final goal is your Lord [...] that it is He who gives death and life. ❜
> *(Qur'an, Surah 53: 36–44)*

Tawrat (Torah)

Whenever the Sahifah are referred to in the Qur'an, the 'scriptures of Musa' are also mentioned. These are better known as the **Tawrat**:

> ❛ We revealed the Torah [Tawrat] with guidance and light, and the prophets, who had submitted to God, judged according to it for the Jews. ❜
> *(Qur'an, Surah 5: 44)*

Muslims believe that the Tawrat contains many good teachings and laws, but was only meant for Jewish people and for a limited time. For Muslims, it is still an important record of the teachings given to Musa. They believe it also includes a prophecy about the future appearance of the Prophet Muhammad:

> ❛ I will raise them up a Navi [Prophet] from among their achim [brothers], like unto thee, and will put My words in his mouth. ❜
> *(Orthodox Jewish Bible, Devarim 18: 18)*

USEFUL TERMS

Injil: original Gospel of Isa
Kutubullah: books of Allah
Revelation: communication from Allah, often through an angel
Sahifah: scrolls of Ibrahim and Moses
Tawrat: Torah
Zabur: Psalms of David

A For Muslims, the Qur'an is the last of Allah's scriptures revealed to humanity

Zabur (Psalms)

Muslims believe the Jewish prophet Dawud (see 1.4) was given the **Zabur**. There are 150 Psalms, made up of songs, prayers, and poems, which Muslims believe were inspired by Allah:

> ❛We have sent revelation to you [Muhammad] as We did to Noah and the prophets after him [...] **to David We gave the book [of Psalms]** [...] They were messengers bearing good news and warning, so that mankind would have no excuse before God, after receiving the messengers❜
> *(Qur'an, Surah 4: 163–165)*

> ❛But the anavim (meek ones) shall inherit Eretz [the earth]; and shall delight themselves in rov shalom (great peace).❜
> *(Orthodox Jewish Bible, Tehillim [Psalms] 37: 11)*

> **SUPPORT** Why would Muslims consider holy scriptures to be more important than other books? Discuss your answer with a partner.

> **STRETCH** Explain what this teaching from the Zabur might mean.

Injil (Gospel)

The **Injil** is the original Gospel taught by Isa. It should not be confused with the four gospels in the New Testament, which are accounts of Isa's life and teaching written by his followers. Muslims believe that part of the Injil of Isa is included in the four gospels but the original became lost, forgotten, or altered. What is preserved is considered a valuable collection of revelations which taught morals such as love and forgiveness:

> ❛We sent Jesus [Isa], son of Mary: We gave him the Gospel and put compassion and mercy into the hearts of his followers.❜
> *(Qur'an, Surah 57: 27)*

> ❛We gave him [Isa] the Gospel with guidance, light, and confirmation of the Torah already revealed – a guide and lesson for those who take heed of God.❜
> *(Qur'an, Surah 5: 46)*

Qur'an

Muslims believe that Allah revealed the Qur'an to the Prophet Muhammad as his final revelation, because previous holy texts had become unreliable. They believe that the Qur'an is the only scripture meant for *all times, all people*, and *all places* because Muhammad was a universal messenger who came at a time when Allah decided the world was ready for his complete message. Muslims believe it contains information that could only have come from Allah:

> ❛Nor could this Qur'an have been devised by anyone other than God. It is a confirmation of what was revealed before it and an explanation of the Scripture. **Let there be no doubt about it, it is from the Lord of the Worlds.**❜
> *(Qur'an, Surah 10: 37)*

> **B** Did you know that the Qur'an and Bible have been rated the world's most popular books?

The Qur'an is described as 'free from any distortion' (Surah 39: 28), 'a blessed Scripture' (Surah 6: 155), 'a mercy' (Surah 29: 51), and 'the most beautiful of all teachings' (Surah 39: 23). Muslims believe that, over 14 centuries after its revelation, the entire text of the Qur'an remains unchanged. This is part of a promise made by Allah (Surah 15: 9).

> **'The Qur'an is nothing less than a revelation that is sent to him [Muhammad].** It was taught to him by [an angel] with mighty powers and great strength [...] [The Prophet's] own heart did not distort what he saw [...] he saw some of the greatest signs of his Lord. **'**
> *(Qur'an, Surah 53: 4–18)*

Write down two reasons why Muslims believe the Qur'an is different from other holy books. **SUPPORT**

Why are Muslim holy books important for Muslims today?

- There is little divergence in the way Muslims view the holy books. All texts prior to the Qur'an are held in high respect by Muslims because they believe they contain messages originally sent by Allah and gave important moral guidance to the people of the time.
- Muslims believe that all the revealed scriptures prepared the way for the final and eternal revelation: the Qur'an. This is the ultimate guide for Muslims today.
- The Prophet Muhammad's wife, 'A'ishah, said that Muhammad was a living example of the Qur'an. Muslims, therefore, try to follow his example by acting according to the Qur'an's teachings.

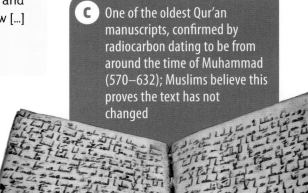

C One of the oldest Qur'an manuscripts, confirmed by radiocarbon dating to be from around the time of Muhammad (570–632); Muslims believe this proves the text has not changed

BUILD YOUR SKILLS

1 Copy and complete the following table to summarize what you know about the holy books.

Book	Prophet	What do we know about its contents?	Why is it important for Muslims?

2 Can an ancient scripture still be relevant today?
   a How would an atheist respond?
   b How would a Muslim respond?
   Make sure you explain your arguments.

SUMMARY

- Muslims believe many holy books came originally from Allah and were for particular societies at particular times.
- Muslims believe that, prior to the Qur'an, holy scriptures were changed or lost, and so needed replacing.
- The Qur'an is believed by Muslims to be the final and perfect revelation for all times, people, and places.

? EXAM-STYLE QUESTIONS

b Explain **two** Muslim attitudes to holy books. (4)
d 'All Muslim holy books are equally important.'
   Evaluate this statement considering arguments for and against. In your response you should:
   - refer to Muslim teachings
   - refer to different Muslim points of view
   - reach a justified conclusion. (15)

1.6 Malaikah

When you hear the word 'angel', what do you imagine? How are angels shown in books and films? Do those depictions reflect how religious believers perceive them?

Muslims believe in angels because they are mentioned in the Qur'an. For Sunni Muslims this belief is one of the six Beliefs (see 1.1).

What is the nature of angels?

Malaikah are beings created by Allah to perform various tasks, particularly governing the universe and the laws of nature. Unlike humans, angels have no free will and can only obey the commands of Allah.

There is a degree of mystery surrounding the nature of angels, which is why Muslims have varying opinions about them. Many Muslims believe that angels do not possess any fixed material form, and therefore cannot be seen physically. However, when they appear to human beings (such as in a vision), they appear in ways which can be imagined by people.

For instance, the angel Jibril (Gabriel) appeared to the Prophet Muhammad in the form of an ordinary human being (see 1.1), and to Isa (Jesus) as a dove.

> ❝ Praise be to God, Creator of the heavens and earth, who made angels messengers with two, three, four [pairs of] wings. ❞
> *(Qur'an, Surah 35: 1)*

In this verse, angels are described as having pairs of wings. While some Muslims would read this literally, others would understand this to be a metaphor for having power or ability.

Angels are believed to help those whose faith is strong:

> ❝ As for those who say, "Our Lord is God," and **take the straight path towards Him, the angels come down to them** and say, "Have no fear or grief, but rejoice in the good news of Paradise, which you have been promised. **We are your allies in this world and in the world to come.**" ❞
> *(Qur'an, Surah 41: 30–32)*

According to Islam, God has created numerous angels in Islam; those who are considered higher in rank are called 'archangels'. They include Jibril, Mika'il (Michael), and Izra'il (Azrael).

SPECIFICATION FOCUS

Malaikah: the nature and importance of angels for Muslims; how angels Jibril, Izra'il and Mika'il are shown in the Qur'an including Surah 19, 32: 11 and 2: 97–98, and their significance for Muslims today

USEFUL TERMS

Kiraman katibin: the noble scribes, the angels who note every person's good and bad deeds

Malaikah: the Arabic name for angels

A **metaphor** is a direct comparison suggesting a resemblance between one thing and another. **SUPPORT**

Read these verses carefully and answer the following questions: **SUPPORT**
- Whom do the angels come down to visit?
- Why do the angels tell them to 'have no fear'?
- What does this passage tell us about the nature of angels?

How are Jibril, Mika'il, and Izra'il shown in the Qur'an?

Jibril

Jibril has a very important role: when Allah wants to communicate with his prophets (see 1.4), he does so through Jibril. It was Jibril who said:

> ❛**We only descend [with revelation] at your Lord's command** – everything before us, everything behind us, everything in between, all belongs to Him. [...] He is Lord of the heavens and earth and everything in between so worship Him: be steadfast in worshipping Him. Do you know of anyone equal to Him?❜
>
> *(Qur'an, Surah 19: 64–65)*

Jibril delivered the whole Qur'an to the Prophet Muhammad over a period of 23 years, starting with the first revelation 'Iqra' ('Read!') (Surah 96: 1–5) when he appeared to the Prophet in the cave of Hira'. Jibril is called 'the Trustworthy Spirit' (Surah 26: 193), which shows how highly Allah values him.

Izra'il

Izra'il is referred to as the angel of death in the Qur'an. He is not referred to by name, but that does not lessen his importance:

> ❛"The Angel of Death put in charge of you will reclaim you, and then you will be brought back to your Lord."❜
>
> *(Qur'an, Surah 32: 11)*

As the 'Angel of Death', Izra'il is responsible for taking the soul of every person and returning it to Allah. However, Muslims believe only Allah knows the time and place of every individual's death.

Mika'il

Mika'il has the responsibility of overseeing the provision and maintenance of life. He is believed to have been placed in charge of the plants and the rain, which Muslim scholars have interpreted more generally to mean that his duties are to provide food for the body (physical) and soul (spiritual).

A The Qur'an says that malaikah comfort believers in their time of need

Jibril and Mika'il are mentioned by name in the Qur'an:

> ❝"if anyone is an enemy of God, His angels and His messengers, of Gabriel [Jibril] and Michael [Mika'il], then God is certainly the enemy of such disbelievers."❞
> *(Qur'an, Surah 2: 98)*

In Islam, as with the prophets, it is essential for Muslims to believe in all the angels and to have respect for them. To oppose them is to oppose Allah.

What is the significance of angels for Muslims today?

- Belief in malaikah is the second most important article of faith for Sunni Muslims. Like Allah, their true nature might not be fully known but they play a crucial role in operating and maintaining the whole universe.
- They help believers in their time of need (Surah 41: 30–32).
- The Qur'an says that angels known as **kiraman katibin** (noble scribes) accompany people. Each person has one angel on the right shoulder and one on the left shoulder. The one on the right takes note of good deeds while the one on the left takes note of bad deeds, which will then be presented to Allah on the Day of Judgement (Surah 82: 10–12). This shows the important role given to angels in helping Allah to decide what happens to every individual in the afterlife.

B Cave Hira', where the Prophet Muhammad was first visited by Jibril. Muslims consider the cave to be blessed

BUILD YOUR SKILLS

1. Summarize how the following angels are shown in the Qur'an. Use a single sentence for each: Jibril, Mika'il, and Izra'il.

2. What effect might the kiraman katibin have on Muslims? Discuss with a partner.

3. Explain what you think is the most important teaching about angels for Muslims.

4. Are metaphors the best way to understand angels? Explain your answer. **STRETCH**

SUMMARY

- Muslims believe malaikah (angels) are heavenly beings created by Allah to perform various tasks.
- Important angels include Jibril, Mika'il, and Izra'il.
- The Qur'an says that angels record every person's good and bad actions, which helps decide their fate. This makes them highly significant for Muslims today.

EXAM-STYLE QUESTIONS

c. Explain **two** reasons why Jibril is important to Muslims. In your answer you must refer to a source of wisdom and authority. (5)

d. 'Angels have no relevance today.'
   Evaluate this statement considering arguments for and against. In your response you should:
   - refer to Muslim teachings
   - reach a justified conclusion. (15)

1.7 Al-Qadr

What is the nature of predestination and why is it important?

Muslims believe that Allah knows everything: he is omniscient (see 1.3). As the creator, Allah has put in place certain laws that govern the universe. Many of these laws are predetermined and unchangeable. This belief is known as **al-Qadr**, or predestination.

> ❝He is the All Knowing Creator: when He wills something to be, His way is to say, "Be" – and it is!❞
> (Qur'an, Surah 36: 81–82)

> ❝It is God who raised up the heavens with no visible supports and then established Himself on the throne; **He has subjected the sun and the moon each to pursue its course for an appointed time; He regulates all things**.❞
> (Qur'an, Surah 13: 2)

A Muslims believe that the orbiting of planets around the Sun has been fixed by Allah and is part of al-Qadr

SPECIFICATION FOCUS

Al-Qadr: the nature and importance of predestination for Muslims; how al-Qadr and human freedom relates to the Day of Judgement, including reference to Sahih Al-Bukhari 78: 685; divergent understandings of predestination in Sunni and Shi'a Islam; the implications of belief in al-Qadr for Muslims today

USEFUL TERMS

Akhirah: life after death, when the Day of Judgement takes place

Al-Qadr: (predestination) belief that Allah has preordained certain things and put in place fixed universal laws

Muslims believe that Allah has also put laws in place for human beings. These include factors which are outside a person's control: for example, the genes that were passed down from their parents, and the social and economic status they were born into. Muslims would say that these things are predestined.

List three other things that humans do not have any control over. **SUPPORT**

Belief in predestination is important to Muslims for several reasons:

- It affirms Allah's omnipotence and his capacity to know everything that there is to know.
- The laws governing the universe are designed for the benefit of humanity.
- Allah's knowledge of all things helps Muslims to understand that everything happens for a reason and is part of Allah's plan.

What is human freedom?

Even though some things are beyond human control, Muslims believe that Allah gave humans free will – they have freedom to choose what to think and how to act. If you are hungry and food is in front of you, for example, you have the choice to eat straight away or to wait until later on.

Human freedom and al-Qadr

Muslims believe that sometimes people's choices are in harmony with God's will, which forms part of al-Qadr. These choices contribute to the realization of God's plan. This does not mean, however, that humans do not have freedom, but that their choices are either in conformity with, or against, God's will:

> ❝The Holy Quran [...] clearly states that **every human being is free to choose between good and evil. However, in relation to religion, there are some spheres of destiny which are predetermined and unchangeable**. They are referred to in the Holy Quran as the Sunnah [practice] of God. One such Sunnah is the destiny that God's messengers will always be victorious❞
> (Mirza Tahir Ahmad, An Elementary Study of Islam)

B Muslims believe humans have been given free will, which allows them to make certain choices – some are more difficult than others!

Muslims believe that God's messengers will always succeed in conveying their message regardless of how powerful their enemies may be. There are several examples of this, such as Musa who prevailed against Fir'awn (Pharaoh), and Dawud who defeated Jalut (Goliath) (see 1.4). However, even though the victory of prophets is promised, people still have the choice to follow or oppose them:

> ❝Say, "Now the truth has come from your Lord: let those who wish to believe in it do so, and let those who wish to reject it do so."❞
> (Qur'an, Surah 18: 29)

> ❝Do the believers not realize that if God had so willed, He could have guided all mankind?❞
> (Qur'an, Surah 13: 31)

This shows that Allah could have taken away human freedom, but he chose not to.

God's will can also be affected by human needs and behaviour. Muslims believe that prayers can move Allah's grace and be granted, as long as they do not conflict with any of his laws. For example, a prayer asking God to heal a sick relative may be granted, but a prayer for a new solar system would probably not!

There are, therefore, several ways in which human freedom and al-Qadr can be understood, and which help to explain why predestination is important to Muslims:

- Allah knows everything that happens in the universe, because he created it.
- Allah has established many 'laws' of nature that are beyond human control – these are predetermined.
- Humans have been given freedom and can choose to do certain things – this is part of Allah's plan.
- Nothing happens without Allah's permission.
- Human intentions and actions, such as prayer, can impact Allah's will.

Explain in no more than 80 words the nature and importance of al-Qadr for Muslims.

STRETCH

How do al-Qadr and human freedom relate to the Day of Judgement?

Muslims believe that Allah is just (see 1.3) and so will judge everyone fairly in the **akhirah** (see 1.8). For instance, nobody can help the particular circumstances into which they are born or raised. Muslims believe Allah will not punish someone simply for being born into a crime-ridden society, and will take everything into account when he is passing judgement.

However, Muslims believe humans are responsible for anything they do outside of these factors: people are free to make their own decisions, and so should be responsible for their actions – good and bad, right and wrong. These will be judged in the afterlife.

 C Muslims believe in both predestination and prayer

What are the implications of belief in al-Qadr for Muslims today?

- Al-Qadr is one of the six Beliefs of Sunni Muslims and also has importance for Shi'a Muslims, therefore no Muslim's faith is complete without it.

- Believing in al-Qadr means that Muslims trust Allah is in control of everything in the universe.

- Al-Qadr has a close connection with the akhirah.

- Muslims are also reminded of Allah's omniscience. This means he knows what has happened, is happening, and will happen. Muslims must therefore be prepared to answer for their deeds in the next life.

BUILD YOUR SKILLS

1 Write three important facts about al-Qadr. **SUPPORT**

2 Find and read Hadith Sahih Al-Bukhari 78: 685. What might this Hadith teach Muslims about human freedom and al-Qadr? **STRETCH**

CASE STUDY: SHI'A MUSLIMS AND PREDESTINATION

Shi'a Muslims reject total predestination. One of the 'Usul ad-Din in Shi'a Islam is Adalat (Divine Justice). It is not fair for Allah to punish or reward someone for something he predestined them to do. Therefore, Shi'as believe that it is logically impossible to believe in total predestination and Mi'ad (Day of Judgement) at the same time because that is a contradiction. Shi'as believe certain things are predestined by Allah, such as lifespan. However, Allah can change your destiny as a result of your actions. For example, Allah may predestine you to live until you are 70 but, according to the Shi'a imams, if you do not maintain a good relationship with your family Allah may reduce your lifespan but if you do maintain a good relationship with your family Allah can increase your lifespan. Allah can change your destiny as a result of your good or bad actions.
(Zameer, Shi'a Muslim)

SUMMARY

- Al-Qadr means predestination and is one of the six Beliefs of Sunni Muslims.

- Muslims believe that there are laws that Allah has determined and fixed in the universe.

- Humans have also been given free will, allowing them to make certain choices which they will be accountable for on the Day of Judgement.

EXAM-STYLE QUESTIONS

b Explain **two** reasons why predestination is an important belief for Muslims. (4)

d 'Al-Qadr and human freedom are incompatible.' Evaluate this statement considering arguments for and against. In your response you should:
- refer to Muslim teachings
- refer to different Muslim points of view
- reach a justified conclusion. (15)

1.8 Akhirah

What are Muslim teachings about life after death?

Muslims believe that our physical life will one day come to an end and that all humans will be raised again in the next life, called akhirah.

> ❛They [non-believers] also say, "What? When we are turned to bones and dust, shall we really be raised up in a new act of creation?" Say, "[Yes] even if you were [as hard as] stone, or iron, or any other substance you think hard to bring to life." **Then they will say, "Who will bring us back?" Say, "The One who created you the first time."**❜
> (Qur'an, Surah 17: 49–52)

Some consider this to be a physical **resurrection**, which is why Muslims are buried and not cremated. Other Muslims say that dead bodies are buried out of respect, and it is just the soul that is taken away and given a new form in the akhirah.

Muslims believe that the soul is immortal (eternal). After death, the angel of death, Izra'il (see 1.6), takes the soul to **barzakh**, which is the stage between death and the time of judgement.

What is the nature of judgement, paradise, and hell?

Islam teaches that human life has a purpose. Muslims believe that each person will be responsible for everything they have chosen to do on earth. Their actions will be recorded by angels, known as kiraman katibin (see 1.6), and then judged by Allah in the akhirah. If Allah is pleased with a person, they will enter jannah, or paradise; if he is not pleased with a person, they may be put in hell, or jahannam.

There is a period of waiting before the resurrection and the Day of Judgement. Some Muslims consider resurrection to be physical and spiritual, while others believe it is only spiritual and that souls will be provided with new bodies in the afterlife

SPECIFICATION FOCUS

Akhirah: Muslim teachings about life after death; the nature of judgement, paradise and hell; how they are shown in the Qur'an, including Surah 17: 49–72; divergent ways in which Muslim teachings about life after death affect the life of a Muslim today

USEFUL TERMS

Barzakh: stage between death and the time of judgement

Resurrection: the belief that humans will be raised again in the next life

A Muslims bury their dead in the ground

How are judgement, paradise, and hell shown in the Qur'an?

Judgement

One of the characteristics of Allah is omniscience; he is all-knowing (see 1.3). Muslims, therefore, believe Allah is aware of everything a person has done, and so he can judge them fairly:

> ❝When the Hour arrives, **on that Day people will be separated**: those who believed and did good deeds will delight in a Garden, while those who disbelieved and denied Our messages and the meeting of the Hereafter will be brought into torment.❞
> *(Qur'an, Surah 30: 14–16)*

'The Hour' refers to the time of judgement in the afterlife. **SUPPORT**

This verse says that on the Day of Judgement, 'people will be separated' – those who did good works and are worthy of jannah will be on one side, and those who disbelieved and are deserving of jahannam will be on the other.

Paradise (jannah)

Jannah is described in the Qur'an as a beautiful and attractive place:

> ❝We do not let the reward of anyone who does good go to waste – they will have Gardens of lasting bliss graced with flowing streams. There they will be adorned with bracelets of gold. There they will wear green garments of fine silk and brocade. There they will be comfortably seated on soft chairs. **What a blessed reward! What a pleasant resting place!**❞
> *(Qur'an, Surah 18: 30–31)*

Hell (jahannam)

Jahannam is shown to be a place of pain and suffering:

> ❝those whose good deeds weigh heavy will be successful, but those whose balance is light will have lost their souls for ever and will stay in Hell – **the Fire will scorch their faces and their lips will be twisted in pain.**❞
> *(Qur'an, Surah 23: 102–104)*

The words 'weigh' and 'balance' show that a person's deeds will be weighed up, as if by weighing scales. A person who is 'light' or lacking in good deeds will go to hell.

The descriptions of paradise as a pleasant resting place and of hell as a fiery place of torture are believed by some Muslims to be a literal truth, but not by all. Many Muslims consider much of the Qur'an's language to be symbolic. They would argue that verses like these speak about the beauties and miseries of the afterlife in a way that humans can relate to but not fully understand. The words used for jahannam, for instance, are intended to highlight the seriousness of not believing in Allah and to dissuade people from committing sins.

Is there a need for the Qur'an's descriptions of hell to be so graphic? Explain your views and consider another perspective. **STRETCH**

Many Muslims believe that jahannam, like jannah, will be forever. Other Muslims argue that hell is only temporary, as Allah is forgiving:

> ❝[...] do not despair of God's mercy. God forgives all sins: He is truly the Most forgiving, the Most merciful.❞
> *(Qur'an, Surah 39: 53)*

> ❝A time will come in jahannam when not a single man would be left in it. Its doors and windows will rattle to the blowing wind.❞
> *(Hadith – Kanzul Ummal)*

Some Muslims use these teachings to argue that all souls will eventually enter paradise once they are pure enough.

How do Muslim teachings about life after death affect the life of a Muslim today?

- Belief in the Day of Judgement is one of the six Beliefs of Sunni Muslims and the five roots of 'Usul ad-Din of Shi'a Muslims, and is, therefore, highly significant. Muslims pray to be given a good afterlife:

> ❝Grant us good things in this world and in the life to come.❞
> *(Qur'an, Surah 7: 156)*

B Would Muslims agree with these depictions of paradise and hell?

- Belief in the akhirah affects how Muslims live and treat others, because they know they will be judged.

> ❝On the Day when We summon each community, along with its leader, those who are given their record in their right hand will read it [with pleasure]. **But no one will be wronged in the least:** those who were blind in this life will be blind in the Hereafter, and even further off the path.❞
> *(Qur'an, Surah 17: 71–72)*

This verse emphasizes that justice will be served in the akhirah, because 'no one will be wronged in the least'. The blindness spoken of is understood to be spiritual, not physical, which teaches Muslims not to read references about the akhirah too literally.

- A Muslim will strive to follow the Qur'an, Sunnah, and the Hadith to the best of their ability, so that they will be judged favourably.

- The promise of paradise for good deeds offers Muslims hope for a better afterlife.

CASE STUDY: A SHI'A PERSPECTIVE

The akhirah has a massive effect on the way I live my life as it overshadows everything I do. I am able to live my life understanding that my existence is not centred around me because there is a world greater than that which I currently experience. Belief in Mi'ad is one of five 'Usul ad-Din. We are taught that our purpose on earth is to worship Allah and the reward for worship is paradise, which is determined on the Day of Resurrection. The Twelve Imams taught that worship is not simply limited to praying, but mostly includes how one conducts oneself. Therefore, following the Imams as well as the Prophets is essential as they also guide us in how to live so that when Mi'ad arrives we are satisfied with how we lived our lives.
(Asad, Shi'a Muslim)

 CASE STUDY: A SUNNI PERSPECTIVE

As a Sunni Muslim, one of my key beliefs is that of the afterlife. I wholeheartedly believe everything I do during my time on earth will affect my standing with Allah, the Most High, and, in turn, my eternal fate. This life is a test. As a result of this, I try my best to live my life in accordance with Islam, following the five pillars and trying to do good for the world around me. I know that every action will be weighed on the Day of Judgement and so I have tried to do things in my life that will help me be the best I can be for this life and the next. This is one of the reasons why I became a teacher. I also enjoy, and take great pride in, charity work – this is encouraged in Islam and holds great reward with Allah. As a mother, Islam tells me that my children may well be my pathway into jannah and so it is important to me to give them a religious upbringing.
(Shelina, Sunni Muslim)

 COMPARE AND CONTRAST

Christianity is the main religious tradition of Great Britain. In your exam, you could be asked to **compare and contrast** Muslim beliefs about life after death with Christian beliefs about life after death. Create a table that explains the similarities and differences between them.

 BUILD YOUR SKILLS

1   How might belief in the Day of Judgement impact the life of a Muslim? Explain in no more than 50 words.   **SUPPORT**

2   Can Allah be both merciful and send someone to hell? Refer to your own views and different Muslim views in your answer.

 SUMMARY

- Muslims believe that all humans will be judged in the afterlife.
- Every person will enter either paradise (jannah) or hell (jahannam), based on how they have lived their life.
- Some Muslims consider resurrection to be physical and spiritual, while others believe it is only spiritual and that souls will be provided with new bodies in the afterlife.

? EXAM-STYLE QUESTIONS

b   Describe **two** differences between Islam and the main religious tradition of Great Britain about the beliefs of paradise and hell. (4)

d   'If there is no akhirah, religious teachings are meaningless.' Evaluate this statement considering arguments for and against. In your response you should:
- refer to Muslim teachings
- refer to different Muslim points of view
- reach a justified conclusion. (15)

Revision

BUILD YOUR SKILLS

Look at the list of 'I can' statements below and think carefully about how confident you are. Use the following code to rate each of the statements. Be honest!

Green – very confident. What is your evidence for this?

Orange – quite confident. What is your target? Be specific.

Red – not confident. What is your target? Be specific.

A self-assessment revision checklist is available on *Kerboodle*

I can...

- List the six Beliefs, making reference to Hadith from Kitab al-iman 1: 4

- Explain how the six Beliefs are understood and expressed in Sunni and Shi'a Muslim communities today

- Explain the importance of the six Beliefs for Muslims

- List the five roots of 'Usul ad-Din and explain where they came from, including reference to Surah 112

- Explain why the five roots of 'Usul ad-Din are important for Sevener and Twelver Shi'a communities

- Describe the characteristics of Allah as shown in the Qur'an: Tawhid, immanence, transcendence, omnipotence, beneficence, mercy, fairness and justice, and Adalat in Shi'a Islam, referring to sources of wisdom and authority

- Explain why the characteristics of Allah are important

- Explain what Risalah (prophethood) is and why it is important for Muslims, including reference to Surah 2: 136

- Explain what the prophets – particularly Adam, Ibrahim, Isma'il, Musa, Dawud, Isa and Muhammad – teach Muslims

- List the Muslim holy books and explain their significance, referring to sources of wisdom and authority

- Give divergent Muslim views about the importance of the holy books for Muslims today

- Explain the nature and importance of malaikah (angels) for Muslims

- Describe how angels Jibril, Izra'il and Mika'il are shown in the Qur'an, including reference to Surah 19, 32: 11 and 2: 97–98

- Explain the significance of angels for Muslims today

- Explain what al-Qadr (predestination) is and why it is important for Muslims

- Explain how al-Qadr and human freedom relate to the Day of Judgement, including reference to Sahih Al-Bukhari 78: 685

- Explain divergent understandings of predestination in Sunni and Shi'a Islam

- Explain the implications of belief in al-Qadr for Muslims today

- Explain Muslim teachings about akhirah (life after death)

- Describe the nature of judgement, paradise and hell, and how these are shown in the Qur'an, including reference to Surah 17: 49–72

- Explain divergent ways in which Muslim teachings about life after death affect the life of a Muslim today

- Compare and contrast Muslim beliefs about life after death with Christian beliefs about life after death

Exam practice

On these exam practice pages you will see example answers for each of the exam question types: **a**, **b**, **c** and **d**. You can find out more about these on pages 6–11.

• Question 'a'

*Question **a** is AO1 – it tests your knowledge and understanding.*

> (a) Outline **three** Muslim beliefs about Allah. (3)

Student response

Muslims believe in Tawhid. They also believe that Allah is kind and compassionate.

Improved student response

Muslims believe that Allah is One (this is known as Tawhid). They also believe that Allah is kind and omnipotent.

 Over to you! Give yourself three minutes on the clock and have a go at answering this question. Remember, an answer to an 'Outline' question does not need to include detailed explanations or reasons. You just need to state three Muslim beliefs about Allah. A mark is awarded for each correct point.

 ✓ WHAT WENT WELL

This is a high level answer. Good and relevant examples are given, with about the right amount of detail, and terminology is used correctly e.g. Tawhid.

 ! HOW TO IMPROVE

The link between Allah and Tawhid could have been made clearer. Also, 'kind and compassionate' may be credited as only one belief because they are very similar so, to ensure maximum marks, the student should choose three distinct beliefs as shown in the improved student response.

• Question 'b'

*Question **b** is AO1 – it tests your knowledge and understanding.*

> (b) Explain **two** ways that a Muslim can show their commitment to their faith. (4)

Student response

There are a number of ways that Muslims can show their commitment. One way is by reading the Qur'an, which is the holy book for Muslims. Another is by naming their children after one of the prophets.

Improved student response

Two ways that a Muslim can show commitment to their faith are:
1 By reciting and understanding the Qur'an, which is the holiest book for Muslims as it is Allah's final revelation and is free from any distortion
2 By naming their children after prophets. This is because, by doing this, the children are encouraged to try to develop similar qualities to the prophet they have been named after.

 Over to you! Give yourself four minutes on the clock and have a go at answering this question. Remember, give two different points and develop each one. You could develop your points by providing an example to support each one. Avoid just repeating an earlier point.

 ✓ WHAT WENT WELL

This is a mid level answer. Reading the Qur'an and naming your children after a prophet are two ways in which Muslims can show their commitment to their faith.

 ! HOW TO IMPROVE

The student needs to develop the answer further, to explain why these are examples of ways in which Muslims can demonstrate commitment to their faith. Have a look at the level of detail given in the improved student response.

• Question 'c'

*Question **c** is AO1 – it tests your knowledge and understanding.*

> (c) Explain **two** reasons why Muhammad is an important prophet. In your answer you must refer to a source of wisdom and authority. (5)

Student response

The Qur'an calls Muhammad the Seal of the Prophets. This means that he is the last messenger, so it is not possible for another messenger to come. The Qur'an is the final message to humanity. It was brought by Muhammad, so there isn't a requirement for anyone else.

Improved student response

Muslims believe that there have been more than 124,000 prophets – including Adam, Musa and Isa. They all demonstrated different qualities – such as justice, love and forgiveness – and Muslims believe that all of these qualities were demonstrated perfectly by the Prophet Muhammad. Furthermore, he brought the Qur'an, which is Allah's final teaching for the whole of humanity, meaning that there is no need for a new message after him. These are reasons why he has been called the 'Seal of the Prophets' (Qur'an, Surah 33: 40).

 Over to you! Give yourself five minutes on the clock and have a go at answering this question. Remember to refer to the Qur'an, Sunnah and/or the Hadith.

 WHAT WENT WELL

This is a low/mid level answer. The student has a clear understanding of the link between Muhammad and the Qur'an being the last scripture.

(!) HOW TO IMPROVE

One of the most important meanings of 'Seal of the Prophets' is that the various qualities of all other messengers were found in Muhammad, which makes him the best example to follow. The question also requires two reasons and reference to a source of wisdom and authority.

• Question 'd'

*Question **d** is both AO1 and AO2 – this tests your knowledge and understanding as well as your ability to evaluate. **d** questions in this section carry an extra three marks for spelling, punctuation and grammar.*

> *(d) 'There are more similarities than differences between Sunni and Shi'a Muslims.'
> Evaluate this statement, considering arguments for and against. In your response you should:
> • refer to Muslim teachings
> • reach a justified conclusion. (15)

Student response

I believe this is a true statement because the basic beliefs of Sunnis and Shi'as are the same – including Tawhid, Risalah, Hajj and many others. Others say that they differ on certain aspects such as who should have led the Muslim community after the Prophet's death and both have developed their own <u>seperate</u> paths because of some fundamental <u>disagrements</u> like the importance given to ahl al-bayt and Sunnis do not accept the authority of Shi'a imams or vice versa and this affects unity within Islam.

 WHAT WENT WELL

This is a mid level answer. The student shows good knowledge and understanding about similarities and differences between Sunni and Shi'a beliefs, and gives reasons why both groups split and the impact this has had ('affects unity'). More than one viewpoint is given, and they make an informed use of key terms.

Improved student response

I believe this is a true statement because the basic beliefs of Sunni and Shi'a Muslims are the same. This is because they have a shared history and both believe in the Qur'an and the prophethood of Muhammad, from where Muslim teachings come. Therefore, tenets such as Tawhid, Risalah and Hajj unite Sunni and Shi'a Muslims, and feature in their main principles of belief, such as the six Beliefs and five roots of 'Usul ad-Din. Sunni and Shi'a Muslims are often seen praying and going on pilgrimage together. This is in the spirit of teachings that promote unity: 'Hold fast to God's rope all together' (Qur'an, Surah 3: 103).

However, they do also differ on certain aspects, such as who should have led the Muslim community after the Prophet's death. Sunni Muslims believe in all four caliphs after the death of Muhammad, but Shi'a Muslims do not accept the first three, and consider Ali to have been the rightful leader of Muslims. As a result of this split, both groups have developed their own <u>separate</u> paths because of some fundamental <u>disagreements</u> – like the importance given to ahl al-bayt. Sunnis do not accept the authority of Shi'a imams, or vice versa. Sunni and Shi'a Muslims also have differences in the way they pray (for instance, Shi'as place a turbah on the ground) and how they conduct marriages and divorces. This affects unity within Islam and has even led to violent clashes, such as in some parts of the Muslim world today. There are also further divisions within the two branches, like in Shi'a Islam where Twelvers and Seveners have separate lines of imams.

Nevertheless, I still believe that there are more similarities than differences between Sunnis and Shi'as because the Five Pillars and six Beliefs of Sunnis are accepted by Shi'as too, and they are generally seen to be united rather than disunited.

 Over to you! Give yourself 15 minutes on the clock and have a go at answering this question. To begin with, read the statement in the question carefully and understand what it is saying. Show accurate understanding about Muslim beliefs and teachings, and use evidence and reasoned judgements. Aim to write five developed points and a conclusion. You cannot get more than six marks if you do not give different viewpoints.

> **!** **HOW TO IMPROVE**
>
> The answer lacks sufficient depth. More detail is needed about why both groups have shared beliefs, about the cause of the split and about the extent to which Sunni and Shi'a Muslims are more similar or different. A justified conclusion is also required – this is provided in the improved student answer opposite. Notice, too, the spelling errors and lack of punctuation in the final sentence. Remember there are three marks allocated to SPaG.

BUILD YOUR SKILLS

In your exams, you'll need to make sure you use religious terminology correctly. Do you know the meaning of the following important terms for this topic?

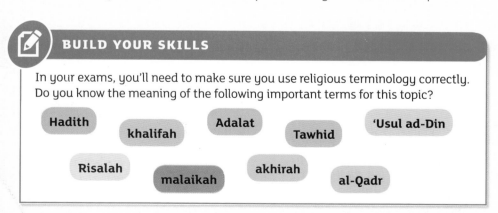

Hadith   khalifah   Adalat   Tawhid   'Usul ad-Din   Risalah   malaikah   akhirah   al-Qadr

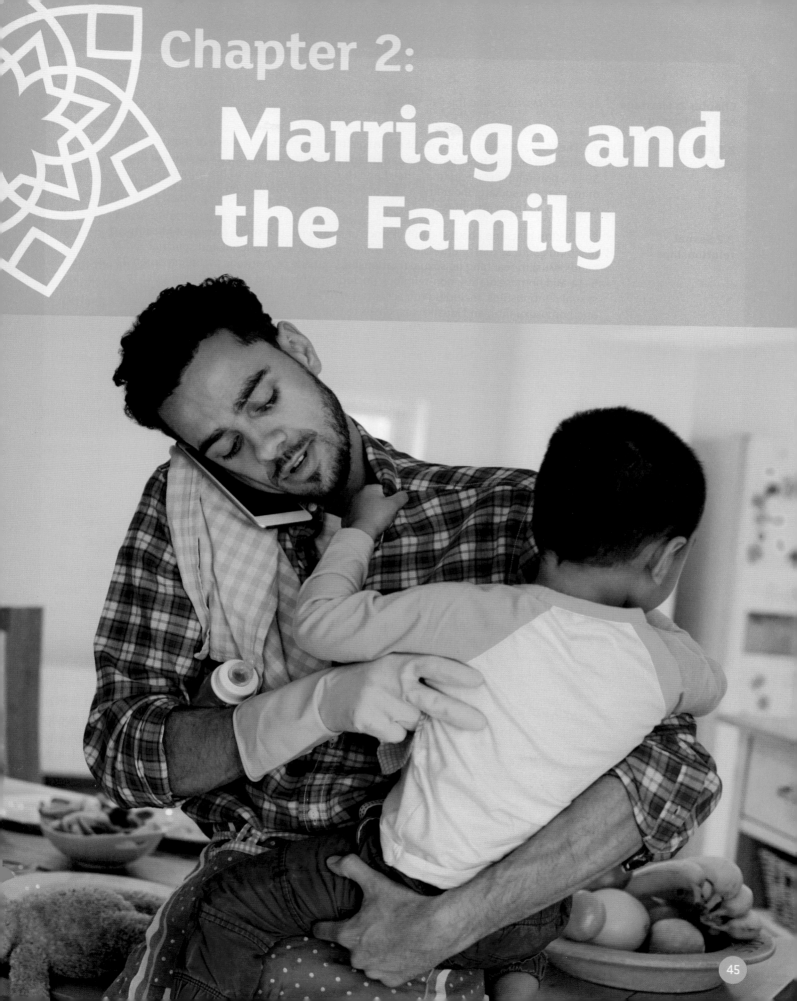

Chapter 2:
Marriage and the Family

Chapter contents	Specification mapping	Page
Chapter 2: Marriage and the Family	Section 2: Marriage and the Family	45
2.1 Marriage	2.1 The importance and purpose of marriage in Islam: the significance of marriage in Muslim life; Muslim teachings about marriage including Surah 4: 1–24 and Surah 24: 30–34; non-religious (including atheist and Humanist) attitudes to the importance of marriage in society; including a lack of importance, cohabitation and the Muslim responses to these attitudes	47
2.2 Sexual relationships	2.2 Muslim teaching about the importance of sexual relationships: divergent Muslim teaching about sexual relationships as fulfilling physical, emotional and spiritual needs; Muslim teaching on sexual relationships outside of marriage including Surah 23: 5–11 and homosexuality; non-religious (including atheist and Humanist) attitudes to sexual relationships, including the acceptance of sexual relationships outside marriage and homosexuality, and Muslim responses to them	49
2.3 The family	2.3 Muslim teaching about the purpose and importance of the family: Muslim teaching about the purpose of families, including Surah 46: 15–18: procreation and the strengthening of the ummah; divergent Muslim responses to the different types of family within 21st-century society (nuclear, single parent, same-sex parents, extended and blended families)	52
2.4 Support for the family	2.4 Support for the family in the ummah: how and why the community tries to support families, including through worship, rites of passage, classes for parents, groups for children and counselling; divergent understandings of the importance of this support for Muslims today and how it might strengthen the ummah, with reference to Surah 3: 102–105	55
2.5 Contraception	2.5 Muslim teaching on contraception: divergent Muslim teachings and attitudes about contraception and family planning, including reference to Sahih Al-Bukhari 34: 432, and 62: 136; different non-religious (including atheist and Humanist) attitudes to family planning and the application of ethical theories, such as situation ethics, and Muslim responses to them	59
2.6 Divorce	2.6 Muslim teaching about divorce: divergent Muslim beliefs, teachings and attitudes towards divorce and remarriage, including Surah 2: 226–241 and the different rules for performing a divorce in Shi'a and Sunni Islam; different non-religious (including atheist and Humanist) attitudes to divorce and remarriage, including the application of ethical theories, such as situation ethics, and Muslim responses to them	61
2.7 Equality of men and women	2.7 Muslim teaching about the equality of men and women in the family: divergent Muslim beliefs, teachings and attitudes about the role of men and women in the family with reference to the Qur'an, including Surah 4 and the time of Muhammad	64
2.8 Gender prejudice and discrimination	2.8 Muslim teaching about gender prejudice and discrimination: Muslim attitudes to gender prejudice and discrimination, including Surah 33: 35; examples of gender equality in action in Islam	67
Revision and Exam Practice	Revision checklist, exam questions, sample answers and guidance	71

Marriage is a recognized union or legal contract between two people who have agreed to commit their lives to each other.

What is the significance of marriage in Muslim life?

In Islam, marriage is known as **nikah**. It is the foundation of a Muslim family. The Prophet Muhammad valued married life:

> ❛Marriage is my Sunnah [practice]. Those who do not follow my practice do not belong to me.❜
> *(Hadith – Sahih Al-Bukhari)*

Marriage is significant to Muslims for many reasons:

- It is considered a religious duty and follows the practice of the Prophet Muhammad.
- It promotes the sharing of love and companionship between two people.
- It acts as a moral safeguard and prevents Muslims from having casual relationships and not treating sex as special.
- It provides a framework for a couple to have children and raise them up in Islam.
- It symbolizes religious and social unity as it brings families, friends, and others together.

What are Muslim teachings about marriage?

Most Muslims marry someone they have known for some time, or have been introduced to by family, friends and also by Muslim matchmaking services. While many Muslim matches are arranged, forced marriages are against Islamic teaching.

> ❛You who believe, it is not lawful for you to inherit women against their will❜
> *(Qur'an, Surah 4: 19)*

Nikah is a solemn and sacred social contract between a man and a woman. The bride must give her consent and is traditionally represented at the ceremony in a mosque by a male guardian, such as her father. In a nikah there is a proposal and an acceptance between bride and groom. In Sunni communities this is in front of at least two witnesses. The groom gives a mahr (dowry) to his bride, as agreed between them.

One of the purposes of human life is **procreation** (see 2.3), which Muslims believe should only happen when a couple is married.

> ❛People, be mindful of your Lord, who created you from a single soul, and from it created its mate, and **from the pair of them spread countless men and women far and wide**❜
> *(Qur'an, Surah 4: 1)*

SPECIFICATION FOCUS

The importance and purpose of marriage in Islam: the significance of marriage in Muslim life; Muslim teachings about marriage including Surah 4: 1–24 and Surah 24: 30–34; non-religious (including atheist and Humanist) attitudes to the importance of marriage in society; including a lack of importance, cohabitation and the Muslim responses to these attitudes

USEFUL TERMS

Cohabitation: living together while not married

Nikah: marriage contract

Procreation: having children

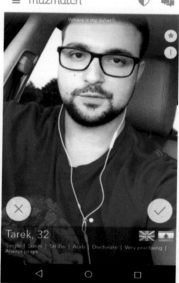

A Matchmaking apps like http://muzmatch.com/ are very popular with single Muslims looking for a life partner

The Qur'an contains many teachings relating to marriage:

> 'you may marry whichever [other] women seem good to you, two, three, or four. If you fear you cannot be equitable [to them], then marry only one'
> *(Qur'an, Surah 4: 3)*

This says Muslim men can marry up to four women, but only if they can treat each wife equally. Due to this teaching, most Muslim men have one wife even if they live in a country where they can have more than one wife. Marriage is considered equal to half of a person's faith.

The Qur'an advises a couple to remain committed to each other and to 'lower their eyes and guard their private parts' (Surah 24: 30–31), which means they should not look lustfully at other men and women.

What are non-religious attitudes to marriage?

Marriage is still popular in the UK, although less so compared to half a century ago (400,000 marriages in England and Wales in 1973 compared to 262,000 in 2012). Changes in social attitudes towards marriage mean that many couples are choosing to **cohabit**, because they do not consider getting married to be very important. However, not all non-religious views about marriage are the same. For many non-religious people, including atheists and Humanists, marriage:

- is a public declaration of a couple's love
- can provide financial and emotional stability for the family
- is not necessary for the expression of love between two people
- can often lead to divorce
- confirms a commitment two people have made to each other
- requires a wedding ceremony which many people cannot afford.

Muslim responses

Muslims oppose alternatives to marriage, like cohabitation, because:

- sex is only permitted within marriage
- marriage helps to protect the couple from any sin and temptations they might face if they were not married
- performing the nikah means the relationship is taken more seriously within marriage.

> 'When a man has married, he has completed one half of his religion.'
> *(Hadith – Tirmidhi)*

What might the Prophet Muhammad have meant by this? **STRETCH**

Separate these into reasons for and against marriage. **SUPPORT**

What other reasons might Muslims give for marriage? Explain your answer. **STRETCH**

BUILD YOUR SKILLS

1 Identify three reasons why Muslims marry. Which purpose do you think is most important, and why? Discuss with a partner.

2 Is marriage necessary to show your love and devotion to somebody? Explain your answer.

EXAM-STYLE QUESTIONS

b Explain **two** reasons why Muslims marry. (4)

d 'Marriage is the most important duty of a Muslim.'
Evaluate this statement considering arguments for and against. In your response you should:
- refer to Muslim teachings
- reach a justified conclusion. (12)

SUMMARY

- Marriage is considered a religious duty in Islam.
- Many non-religious people, including atheists and Humanists, support marriage, but others think it is unnecessary and believe cohabitation is sufficient.

2.2 Sexual relationships

What are Muslim teachings about sexual relationships?

Islam recognizes the need for sex as an expression of love and a means of having children. Sexual relationships help fulfil physical, emotional, and spiritual needs. Muslims believe these relationships should only take place within marriage.

Physical

Sexual desire is natural and Muslims are taught that it is best fulfilled within marriage.

> ❛Another of His [Allah's] signs is that He created spouses from among yourselves for you to live in tranquillity: He ordained love and kindness between you❜
> *(Qur'an, Surah 30: 21)*

Emotional

The Qur'an teaches that by committing themselves to each other, both husband and wife become a means of comfort for each other:

> ❛they are [close] as garments to you, as you are to them.❜
> *(Qur'an, Surah 2: 187)*

A garment helps to cover the body and is a source of protection. This is how a couple should support each other.

Spiritual

Muslims believe that marriage provides an individual with a soulmate for life. Therefore, their relationship is not only physical and emotional, but spiritual too:

> ❛"Our Lord, give us joy in our spouses and offspring. Make us good examples to those who are aware of You".❜
> *(Qur'an, Surah 25: 74)*

In this prayer, a couple are asking Allah to make them a model of excellent moral conduct for others to look up to.

SPECIFICATION FOCUS

Muslim teaching about the importance of sexual relationships: divergent Muslim teachings about sexual relationships as fulfilling physical, emotional and spiritual needs; Muslim teaching on sexual relationships outside of marriage including Surah 23: 5–11 and homosexuality; non-religious (including atheist and Humanist) attitudes to sexual relationships, including the acceptance of sexual relationships outside marriage and homosexuality, and Muslim responses to them

USEFUL TERMS

Adultery: sex where one or both of those involved are already married to someone else (extramarital sex)

Homosexuality: sexual relations between two people of the same sex

Premarital sex: a sexual relationship which occurs before marriage

A Muslims are taught that a marital relationship should be affectionate in every sense

What are Islamic teachings on sexual relationships outside of marriage?

The Qur'an and the Hadith forbid **premarital sex**, as it takes place outside marriage. It is viewed as a serious sin:

> ❛"stay well away from committing obscenities, whether openly or in secret"❜
> *(Qur'an, Surah 6: 151)*

Muslims believe that any situation that could lead to sin should be avoided. Islam encourages modest dress, and discourages boys and girls mixing freely, particularly when they reach puberty. The Prophet Muhammad said that if a man and woman who are not related are left alone, Satan joins them, meaning they might be tempted to sin. Therefore, Muslims are taught to 'guard their chastity' (purity) (Surah 23: 5).

Adultery

Adultery is also condemned by God in the Qur'an, and the punishment laid down for it is severe:

> ❛And do not go anywhere near adultery: it is an outrage, and an evil path.❜
> *(Qur'an, Surah 17: 32)*

> ❛Strike the adulteress and the adulterer one hundred times. Do not let compassion for them keep you from carrying out God's law – if you believe in God and the Last Day – and ensure that a group of believers witness the punishment.❜
> *(Qur'an, Surah 24: 2)*

There are strict conditions for this. For example, four witnesses must have seen the act of adultery in order for the punishment to apply (Surah 24: 13).

Adulterers are punished in some Muslim countries, such as Saudi Arabia, but many Muslims believe that Allah will forgive an adulterer and adulteress if they are sincere in their repentance.

What are Islamic teachings on homosexuality?

Islam teaches that the act of **homosexuality** is a sin; it is regarded as unnatural and goes against Allah's will. One of the purposes of human creation is to reproduce, and this is not possible in a homosexual relationship.

Muslim attitudes towards homosexuality are based on the story of the Prophet Lot, who was upset with people in his society because of their sexual acts:

> ❛We sent Lot and he said to his people, **"How can you practise this outrage? No other people has done so before. You lust after men rather than women!** You transgress all bounds!" […] and We showered upon [the rest of] them a rain [of destruction].❜
> *(Qur'an, Surah 7: 80–84)*

B Many Muslims believe that Allah can forgive a person who repents of their sin

STRETCH
Do you think people should be punished for committing adultery? Give reasons for your opinion and explain why someone would disagree with you. What do you think a Muslim would argue?

SUPPORT
Lot is criticizing men for wanting to have sexual relationships with other men. Allah punished them by destroying the region and those in it, apart from Lot and his followers.

In many Muslim countries, such as Iran, homosexuality is a crime and punished in the same way as adultery. In other Muslim countries, such as Turkey and Indonesia, homosexuality is not illegal, but people of the same sex are not allowed to marry. In the UK, homosexuality is legal and homosexual couples are permitted to marry.

What are non-religious attitudes to sexual relationships?

Many non-religious people, including atheists and Humanists, say that people should make informed and responsible choices when it comes to sexual relationships. They argue that social attitudes in the UK have changed significantly, and that:

- traditional views and religious beliefs about sex are no longer relevant
- adultery is not illegal
- premarital sex allows people to see if they are physically compatible
- homosexuality is natural and same-sex marriages are now legal
- opposing homosexuality can lead to intolerance and homophobia
- the availability of contraception allows individuals to make sensible decisions about their sex lives.

Muslim responses

- Many Muslims see the rise in sexual relationships outside marriage as unhealthy for society.
- Punishments given in Islam reflect how sinful some sexual acts are.
- Some Muslims believe that certain teachings about sexual relationships should not apply today. They would, for example, support LGBT Muslims in their community. LGBT Muslims are also often seen at Pride events around the country.

> What do the laws in different Muslim countries **SUPPORT** say about attitudes towards homosexuality?

C Broadcaster Stephen Fry and his partner, Elliott Spencer, married in 2015. As of 2013, same-sex couples can legally marry in the UK

D Muslim LGBT activists at a London Pride event in 2005

BUILD YOUR SKILLS

1 Create a revision summary that shows Muslim attitudes to premarital, extramarital, and homosexual relationships.

2 Explain why Islam has laid down strict conditions for the punishment of sexual relationships outside marriage. Refer to at least two teachings.

3 Do you think that there is any kind of sexual relationship that is unacceptable? Explain your reasons. **STRETCH**

SUMMARY

- Islam teaches sex should only take place within marriage and fulfils physical, emotional, and spiritual needs.
- Muslim attitudes to homosexuality are based on the story of the Prophet Lot.

EXAM-STYLE QUESTIONS

b Explain **two** reasons why Muslims are against sexual relationships outside marriage. (4)

d 'You cannot be a Muslim and be in a homosexual relationship.'
Evaluate this statement considering arguments for and against. In your response you should:
- refer to Muslim teachings
- refer to different Muslim points of view
- reach a justified conclusion. (12)

What are Muslim teachings about the purpose of families?

In Islam, the family is at the heart of the Muslim community and the foundation of society. It is the most important way of ensuring that children grow up as good, faithful Muslims. For this purpose, Muslims are encouraged to marry within Islam. The Prophet Muhammad said that the most important element to look for in a life partner is their religion:

> ❝A women is married for four [reasons]: her wealth, her family [status], her beauty, and her religion. Choose a religious woman, you will prosper.❞
> *(Hadith – Sahih Al-Bukhari)*

Islam promotes love and kindness between members of the family at all levels:

> ❝The best of you is the one who behaves best towards the members of his family❞
> *(Hadith – Tirmidhi)*

This Hadith highlights the importance of treating close relatives well. Muslims believe that each member of the family has certain roles and responsibilities, and also rights, that need to be honoured. This is so that a home can be as harmonious as possible.

Mothers and fathers have a crucial part to play in raising children and preparing the next generation of Muslims. This is why the Qur'an has explained the importance of giving parents respect, particularly mothers:

> ❝We have commanded man to be good to his parents – his mother struggled to carry him and struggled to give birth to him; his bearing and weaning took a full thirty months❞
> *(Qur'an, Surah 46: 15)*

Muslims are also taught to pray for their parents:

> ❝"Lord, help me to be grateful for Your favours to me and my parents."❞
> *(Qur'an, Surah 46: 15)*

> ❝Paradise lies at the feet of your mothers❞
> *(Hadith – Nasa'i)*

Here, the Prophet Muhammad is saying that by serving one's mother, a Muslim can attain paradise.

SPECIFICATION FOCUS

Muslim teaching about the purpose and importance of the family: Muslim teaching about the purpose of families, including Surah 46: 15–18: procreation and the strengthening of the ummah; divergent Muslim responses to the different types of family within 21st-century society (nuclear, single parent, same-sex parents, extended and blended families)

Why do you think the Prophet Muhammad said faith was the most important thing to find in a partner? List ways this could benefit family life. **STRETCH**

A A Muslim family

Procreation

Islam teaches that one of the purposes of human life is procreation, therefore married couples are expected to have children, if they are able to. How children are brought up and treated will also impact on their personal development, so it is important to ensure they are given the best possible care:

> ❝Honour your children and make provisions for their proper upbringing❞
> *(Hadith – Ibn Majah)*

Children are taught important etiquette, and many parents also arrange for their children to attend classes at a mosque or madrasah (Islamic school) to learn more about their faith.

Strengthening of the ummah

Raising children properly is a way of strengthening the **ummah**, the community of Muslims around the world. Muslim parents consider their role extremely important in ensuring that children continue their religious practices and traditions, and in helping to make the Muslim community grow and become stronger.

These teachings are also important to Muslims today because:

- they remind Muslims how much Allah cares about families
- Muslims believe they provide an ideal to aspire to, and are the key to a harmonious home
- Muslims believe Muhammad was the best example to follow of how to treat relatives
- they can be consulted in times of difficulty in order to resolve any issues.

Muslims believe they have a responsibility to protect family values at a time when marriage is in decline and other types of family are becoming more popular. Upholding Muslim values is also a way of strengthening the ummah.

What are Muslim responses to different types of family in today's society?

Nuclear and extended families

A **nuclear** family is also known as a 'traditional family' where a mother, father, and their children all live together as a unit. Most Muslims place the greatest value on this type of family as this is how the Prophet Muhammad lived.

An extended family includes the nuclear family, and the couple's parents, aunts and uncles, or cousins, all living nearby or together. This is common in many Muslim families due to the importance given to caring for one's parents and other relatives.

Single-parent families

This is when one parent dies or a parent divorces or separates from their partner and becomes responsible for any children. Most Muslims would prefer that the parent not remain single as they believe both a mother and a father are required

B The Prophet Muhammad taught that paradise is the reward for those who respect and serve their mothers

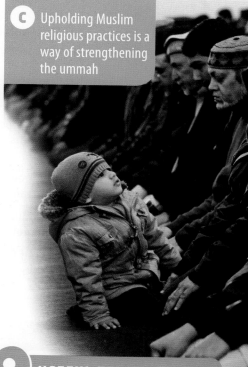

C Upholding Muslim religious practices is a way of strengthening the ummah

USEFUL TERMS

Blended family: two families uniting when parents meet new partners

Nuclear family: mother, father, and children living as one unit

Surrogacy: when a woman becomes pregnant and gives birth for a couple who are unable to have children

Ummah: community of Muslims around the world

to ensure a proper upbringing for the children. Where this is not possible, members of the local Muslim community will offer emotional, financial, and spiritual support to the family. Some single-parent Muslims believe that they do not need, and are happier without, a partner.

Same-sex parents

This is when a homosexual couple become parents, through either adoption or **surrogacy**. Muslims oppose this family type as they believe that Allah created man to be with woman (see 2.2).

Blended families

Blended or reconstituted families are formed when two or more sets of children (stepbrothers and stepsisters) become one family when one or both of their parents meet someone new. Most Muslims would agree that blended families are better than single-parent families as they bring two groups of people together.

D Actor Will Smith is part of a blended family

BUILD YOUR SKILLS

1 Produce a revision mind-map or poster showing the purpose and importance of family life for Muslims. Include and explain examples of Muslim teachings.

2 With a partner, choose any three Muslim teachings about family life that you feel are especially important today. Explain your selection.

3 Are religious beliefs about family life still relevant in twenty-first-century Britain? Consider what a non-religious person might say and why.

4 'Many Muslim teachings about family life are impractical.'
Do you agree? Explain your answer.   **STRETCH**

SUMMARY

- There are many different types of family.
- The family is at the heart of the Muslim community and the foundation of society.
- There are many teachings in Islam about the importance of family life.
- Procreation and the strengthening of the ummah are two purposes of family.

EXAM-STYLE QUESTIONS

a State **three** types of family. (3)
c Explain **two** reasons why family is important for Muslims. In your answer you must refer to a source of wisdom and authority. (5)

2.4 Support for the family

Community is very important in Islam. Muslims are part of the ummah (community), which makes them feel part of a global family, made up of brothers and sisters in religion. There are many support services that Muslim communities offer, often in a mosque. A family's visit to the mosque fulfils a spiritual and social purpose.

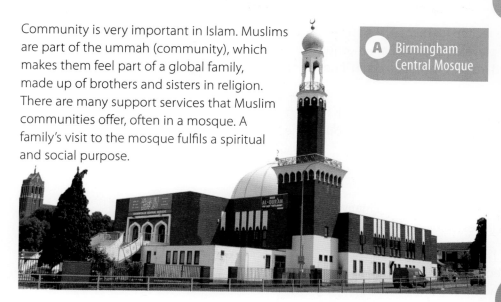

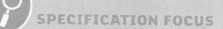

A Birmingham Central Mosque

SPECIFICATION FOCUS

Support for the family in the ummah: how and why the community tries to support families, including through worship, rites of passage, classes for parents, groups for children and counselling; divergent understandings of the importance of this support for Muslims today and how it might strengthen the ummah, with reference to Surah 3: 102–105

How and why does the community try to support families?

There are a number of activities, events, and services that communities run, organize, and offer to local people.

Worship

Muslims are encouraged to pray in mosques, as they are the houses of Allah. The mosque is often described as the beating heart of the local Muslim community. It is the spiritual home for Muslims who try to attend the mosque regularly to offer their daily prayers. This helps everyone feel part of the ummah.

Rites of passage

These are points – usually marked by a ceremony – when an individual makes a transition from one phase of life to another. In Islam, there are a number of rites of passage:

- Birth: When a baby is born, the **adhan** – which includes the shahadah (see 3.2) – is recited into the right ear, usually by the father. This means that the first words a baby hears are about Allah. The baby is given something sweet and parents may chew a little piece of date and rub the juice onto the baby's gums, as this was the practice of the Prophet Muhammad. It is believed that this helps the digestive system get started.

- **Aqiqah:** This usually takes place on the seventh day after birth. The baby's scalp is shaved of hair to represent cleanliness and to symbolize dedication to God. The hair is weighed and its equivalent in gold or silver is given to charity. Animals are also sacrificed and the meat is distributed to family, friends and the poor. A celebration dinner is held for family and friends to welcome the child into the world.

USEFUL TERMS

Adhan: the call to prayer in Arabic

Aqiqah: a ceremony marking the birth of a newborn baby

Khitan: male circumcision, when a baby's foreskin is removed for health reasons

Shari'ah: Islamic legal system based on Muslim scholars' understanding of the Qur'an, Sunnah and the Hadith

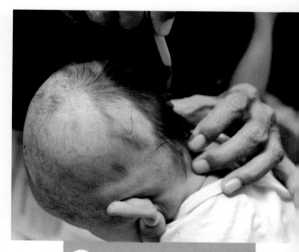

B The aqiqah ceremony where a baby's scalp is shaved

- **Khitan:** This means circumcision and involves the removal of a baby boy's foreskin for the purpose of cleanliness and sexual purity later in life. This ritual usually takes place within seven days of the birth. Khitan is based on a religious tradition started by the Prophet Ibrahim.
- **Death:** When a person dies, prayers are recited for them. The body is washed and then shrouded in white. A funeral prayer is offered at the mosque or cemetery, and when the body is buried (usually without a coffin if possible) it must face Makkah.

The community takes an active part in all of these rituals to share both the joys and sorrows that fellow Muslims experience in life. This helps to strengthen the social and spiritual bond in the ummah.

Classes for parents

In Islam, seeking knowledge is a form of worship. This is why in many mosques there will be a library, bookshop, regular classes, study circles, and talks for young and old, men and women.

Classes are offered for parents (who are segregated into male and female groups), which focus on enhancing their understanding about Islam and studying the meaning of the Qur'an. They are also opportunities for parents to discuss issues or challenges they may be facing in raising their children, especially in a non-Muslim society. Sometimes a visiting speaker will be invited to offer specialist advice based on the teachings of the Qur'an, Sunnah, and the Hadith.

Groups for children

Classes are also run for children, from those in nursery to students doing their GCSEs. Boys and girls are usually taught separately. Classes aim to develop the children's knowledge of Muslim beliefs and practices, and how to become good citizens. They are usually led by an imam or knowledgeable person.

Many Muslim communities run competitions at local, regional, and national levels for reciting the Qur'an and religious poems, making speeches, and team quizzes.

Some mosques also have recreational and sporting facilities, such as a gym and sports hall where badminton, indoor cricket, table tennis, and even tug of war are organized regularly and for free. Girls may also have the opportunity to take part in arts and crafts and cookery lessons at the mosque.

These activities aim to make coming to the mosque both an educational and enjoyable experience for families, and bring the community closer together.

Counselling

The mosque plays a key role in maintaining peace within homes and in the community. Mosque leaders are often involved in resolving problems in personal relationships or between families. This is why many mosques have family support services, counselling clinics, and **shari'ah** councils.

C Members of a shari'ah council hear a divorce case

❝The believers are brothers, so make peace between your two brothers and be mindful of God, so that you may be given mercy.❞
(Qur'an, Surah 49: 10)

Some Muslim communities arrange premarital counselling sessions to offer advice on the rights and responsibilities that come with marriage, and to give couples a chance to talk frankly about their compatibility and whether their marriage could work. They believe this can help avoid problems arising later on, like divorce.

SUPPORT

Why do you think the Qur'an has used the word 'brothers' for Muslims who are not biologically related?

STRETCH

Copy out this verse and explain whether or not you think it can help to prevent family problems.

CASE STUDY: BIRMINGHAM CENTRAL MOSQUE

The Mosque organizes:

- family support services and a counselling clinic
- marriage services, such as a marriage bureau, events and marriage registration
- funerals
- open days and school visits
- educational classes
- a sports forum promoting sporting activities for young Muslims.

D Birmingham Central Mosque hosts many events and services to support Muslim families and the community

Why is community support important to Muslims today?

> ❛**Hold fast to God's rope all together**; do not split into factions [...] Be a community that calls for what is good, urges what is right, and forbids what is wrong: those who do this are the successful ones. Do not be like those who, after they have been given clear revelation, split into factions and fall into disputes❜
> *(Qur'an, Surah 3: 103–105)*

Muslims believe there is strength in unity; that if they 'hold fast to God's rope', they will stay and grow as one community (see 2.3). The support given by the ummah also:

- provides ways for Muslims to learn more about their faith
- helps to resolve issues and problems by involving trusted people
- gives Muslims a sense of identity and belonging, particularly at a time when many Muslims feel targeted in the media and in society due to negative attitudes towards Islam.

The extent to which Muslim communities can offer support to families is often dependent on the size of the local Muslim community and the facilities available at the mosque.

BUILD YOUR SKILLS

1   Give two examples of the value of a local community.

SUPPORT

2   Read the case study about Birmingham Central Mosque.
   a   Which Muslim teachings is the Birmingham Central Mosque fulfilling? Write down two examples with an explanation for each.
   b   How and why do mosque communities like the Birmingham Central Mosque try to help families and local people? Produce a short advert for a local newspaper promoting a mosque's services.

SUMMARY

- The Muslim community provides a range of support services for the benefit of local people.
- Many mosques arrange educational classes and counselling sessions for families.

EXAM-STYLE QUESTIONS

b   Outline **three** ways that the Muslim community helps families. (3)
c   Explain **two** reasons why the provision of counselling is important for Muslims. In your answer you must refer to a source of wisdom and authority. (5)

Forms of **contraception** are used to avoid pregnancy. A couple may use contraceptives if they decide not to have children, or if they wish to wait before they do. This is called **family planning**.

What are Muslim teachings and attitudes about contraception and family planning?

There are very few direct teachings about contraception in the Qur'an, Sunnah, or the Hadith, so Muslim scholars use key principles from these sources to form beliefs and attitudes about its use.

Islam is pro-life and regards children as a blessing (see 2.3). Therefore, any form of birth control is considered to be interfering with Allah's plan because it prevents a life from developing.

> ❛God has control of the heavens and the earth; **He creates whatever He will** – He grants female offspring to whoever He will, male to whoever He will, or both male and female, and He makes whoever He will barren: He is all knowing and all powerful. ❜
> *(Qur'an, Surah 42: 49–50)*

> ❛Do not kill your children for fear of poverty – We shall provide for them and for you – killing them is a great sin. ❜
> *(Qur'an, Surah 17: 31)*

Many Muslims interpret this teaching as prohibiting birth control if it is for financial reasons, because Allah is the provider.

However, there are Muslims who believe that temporary and reversible forms of contraception are acceptable within marriage, particularly just after the birth of a child:

> ❛Mothers suckle their children for two whole years, if they wish to complete the term [...] **No one should be burdened with more than they can bear**: no mother shall be made to suffer harm on account of her child, nor any father on account of his. ❜
> *(Qur'an, Surah 2: 233)*

Some Muslim scholars have interpreted this verse to mean that there should be a two-year gap between the birth of one child and the next. Within this time, sex is not denied to the couple and the use of contraception is acceptable.

SPECIFICATION FOCUS

Muslim teaching on contraception: divergent Muslim teachings and attitudes about contraception and family planning, including reference to Sahih Al-Bukhari 34: 432, and 62: 136; different non-religious (including atheist and Humanist) attitudes to family planning and the application of ethical theories, such as situation ethics, and Muslim responses to them

USEFUL TERMS

Coitus interruptus: when the penis is removed from the vagina before ejaculation

Contraception: the deliberate prevention of pregnancy

Family planning: when a couple consider whether or not to have a child

Situation ethics: the idea that people should base moral decisions on what is the most loving thing to do

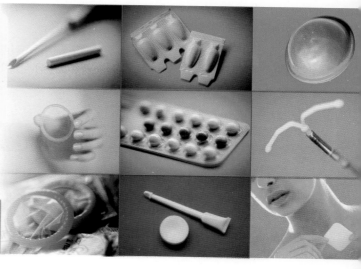

A Modern artificial contraceptives come in a variety of forms

Hadiths in Sahih Al-Bukhari (34: 432 and 62: 136) show that when the Prophet Muhammad was asked his opinion about **coitus interruptus**, an early withdrawal method of contraception, he expressed his disapproval but did not forbid it:

> ❝Do you really do that? It is better for you not to do it.❞
> *(Hadith – Sahih Al-Bukhari 34: 432)*

Muslims may also justify the use of contraceptives:

- if pregnancy could result in the mother's death
- to save conceiving a child that might inherit an illness from a parent
- if they feel couples should be able to make their own decisions about the size of their family.

Permanent forms of contraception are generally prohibited except where a woman's health or life may be in danger if she conceives.

What are non-religious attitudes to family planning?

- Non-religious people, including atheists and Humanists, do not believe in God, and so do not consider religious beliefs and teachings about contraception and family planning as relevant.
- Contraception and family planning enable a couple to express their love for each other without the possibility of having children. This includes people who are not financially or emotionally ready for parenthood.
- Many adults may not want to have children until later, but still wish to have an active sex life. Certain types of contraception, such as condoms, can help to prevent sexually transmitted infections from spreading.

Some ethical theories adopt a particular principle or rule when making moral decisions. **Situation ethics** focuses on the law of love as the best way of deciding what to do in particular circumstances. A question that a situation ethicist would therefore ask about family planning is: 'Is it the most loving thing for everyone involved?'

Muslim responses

Some Muslims share some non-religious attitudes to family planning, especially when a couple might be too young to take on parenting responsibilities. However, Muslims consider children to be a blessing from Allah, who will remove any worries about the cost of bringing up a child.

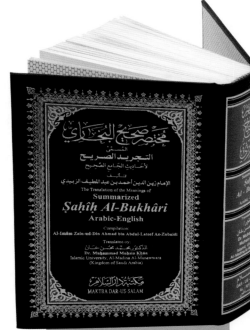

B Muslims look towards books of Hadith, such as Sahih Al-Bukhari, for guidance on family planning issues

BUILD YOUR SKILLS

1 Explain the difference between contraception and family planning. **SUPPORT**

2 Identify two circumstances when Muslims may accept the use of contraception, and two when they would not.

3 Is using contraception a form of killing? Give reasons for your opinion. **STRETCH**

SUMMARY

- In Islam, life is a gift from Allah and contraception interferes with this.
- Most Muslims believe contraception is allowed for specific reasons, such as child-spacing, but only within marriage.
- Many non-religious people, and some Muslims, believe that contraception is acceptable when a couple are not ready for a child.

EXAM-STYLE QUESTIONS

a Outline **three** Muslim attitudes towards family planning. (3)

b Explain **two** reasons why Muslims may accept the use of contraception. (4)

2.6 Divorce

What are Muslim beliefs, teachings, and attitudes towards divorce and remarriage?

There are many verses in the Qur'an that deal with the issue of **divorce** and **remarriage**. Muslim beliefs and attitudes are also based on the Hadith and various rulings from Islamic scholars.

Marriage is important in Islam (see 2.1). Islam seeks to bring and keep people together – anything that leads to separation is seen as breaking a link that Allah created:

> ❝Of all the things Allah has made lawful, He hates talaq [divorce] the most❞
> *(Hadith – Abu Dawud)*

However, there are circumstances when maintaining a marriage becomes very difficult, disagreements cannot be resolved, and divorce seems the only option. This is one reason why, as the above Hadith says, Allah has made it lawful.

Muslims can divorce for a number of reasons, including:

- unfaithfulness
- abuse
- apostasy (leaving Islam).

There are also reasons for annulling a marriage. **Annulment** is not the same as divorce. It can happen for the following reasons:

- a husband being absent for a long time without keeping in touch
- not being able to have children naturally.

Either the husband or the wife can initiate a divorce. The process involves three main steps: initiation, reconciliation, and completion.

Initiation

A husband wishing to divorce his wife must say 'I divorce you' to her three times. Opinions differ about whether the words are allowed to be said on the same occasion, or require a gap between each announcement. In Shi'a Islam there must be a gap, which most Sunnis also believe. This is to ensure that no hasty decision is made. A wife can initiate a divorce without making this announcement.

Reconciliation

In the event of a disagreement or dispute between the couple, the Qur'an encourages them to try to reconcile and reach a peaceful resolution, as 'peace is best' (Surah 4: 128).

SPECIFICATION FOCUS

Muslim teaching about divorce: divergent Muslim beliefs, teachings and attitudes towards divorce and remarriage, including Surah 2: 226–241; and the different rules for performing a divorce in Shi'a and Sunni Islam; different non-religious (including atheist and Humanist) attitudes to divorce and remarriage, including the application of ethical theories, such as situation ethics, and Muslim responses to them

USEFUL TERMS

Annulment: when it is declared that a marriage was never valid

Divorce: legally ending a marriage

Remarriage: marrying again after being divorced from a previous marriage

A Some marriages hit difficult times – Islam allows divorce in some circumstances

Completion

If all efforts at reconciliation fail, a divorce takes place. For a woman wanting a divorce, a shari'ah council (see 2.4) will look into the case on her behalf, as she is often the more vulnerable person in the marriage, and it is important that her rights are properly protected. In Shi'a Islam, two witnesses are required at a divorce.

If the marriage has been consummated (sex has taken place) then the mahr (dowry) must be paid in full by the husband; but if divorce takes place without consummation having occurred, the husband is required to give half the mahr.

Men are reminded to treat the women they divorce with respect:

> ❝When you divorce women and they have reached their set time, then either keep or release them in a fair manner. **Do not hold on to them with intent to harm them and commit aggression:** anyone who does this wrongs himself. ❞
> *(Qur'an, Surah 2: 231)*

> Do you think it is right for a man to pay the mahr when a couple divorce? Be ready to feed back your views to the rest of the class.
>
> **SUPPORT**

Remarriage

The Qur'an guides Muslims on remarriage (Surah 2: 226–241). If a person divorces, they are encouraged to remarry because companionship is considered natural and important in Islam.

A husband and wife who have divorced once or twice (by the husband pronouncing the talaq) may get back together if they wish. However, if the husband pronounces the third talaq then they cannot get back together until the wife has married someone else:

> ❝she will not be lawful for him until she has taken another husband; if that one divorces her, there will be no blame if she and the first husband return to one another❞
> *(Qur'an, Surah 2: 230)*

B A couple receiving marriage counselling

What are non-religious attitudes to divorce and remarriage?

Many non-religious people, including atheists and Humanists, share the view that marriage is a serious and lifelong commitment. Divorce is usually opposed because many problems in relationships can be resolved with counselling, and divorce can cause distress for families and any children from the marriage.

However, non-religious people accept that divorce and remarriage occur for various reasons. They believe:

- marriages do not always work
- people should have the freedom to make decisions about their relationships
- individuals should have the chance to find love again.

Situation ethics focuses on the law of love as the best way of deciding what to do in particular circumstances. A question that a situation ethicist would therefore ask about divorce is: 'Is it the most loving thing for everyone involved?'

CASE STUDY: A SITUATION ETHICS PERSPECTIVE ON DIVORCE

Divorce is always difficult and fraught. However, it can be useful if one partner has fallen out of love with the other or when domestic violence is involved. Remarriage is a vital way of families reforming. It allows for divorced couples to rededicate themselves to their new spouse and helps the children from both "old" marriages to unify.
(Peter Covington, author)

Would Muslims agree with Peter's view? Explain your answer. **STRETCH**

Muslim responses

- Islam recognizes that marriages sometimes fail, and that people will divorce and want to remarry.

- Couples should not enter into a divorce lightly and should think carefully about the consequences and the effect it will have on themselves and their children. For this reason, the Qur'an advises couples to try to reconcile.

- Remarriage should be to a fellow Muslim as faith is an important part of a relationship and family life.

BUILD YOUR SKILLS

1   Identify and explain three reasons why divorce is allowed in Islam.

2   Draw a Venn diagram comparing Muslim and non-religous attitudes to divorce. Label each oval and note the appropriate details in them – the ones that are acceptable to both Muslims and non-religious people should appear in the overlap.

SUPPORT

SUMMARY

- The Qur'an teaches Muslims to resolve disagreements peacefully and that divorce should be the last resort.

- Remarriage is encouraged because of the value of companionship in Islam.

- Non-religious people also believe that divorce is sometimes unavoidable and individuals should have the chance to find love again.

EXAM-STYLE QUESTIONS

a   Outline **three** Muslim beliefs about remarriage. (3)

c   Explain **two** reasons why divorce is allowed in Islam. In your answer you must refer to a source of wisdom and authority. (5)

2.7 Equality of men and women

The Qur'an teaches that men and women were created from one entity, and that together they have a role in procreating:

> ❝ People, be mindful of your Lord, who created you from a single soul, and from it created its mate, and **from the pair of them spread countless men and women far and wide** ❞
>
> *(Qur'an, Surah 4: 1)*

SPECIFICATION FOCUS

Muslim teaching about the equality of men and women in the family: divergent Muslim beliefs, teachings and attitudes about the role of men and women in the family with reference to the Qur'an, including Surah 4, and the time of Muhammad

What are Muslim beliefs, teachings, and attitudes about the role of men and women in the family?

The role of men

The Qur'an teaches that men should marry and that they have responsibility for supporting their family – for housing and feeding them, and for covering the cost of everyday living:

> ❝ Husbands should take good care of their wives, with [the bounties] God has given to some more than others and with what they spend out of their own money. ❞
>
> *(Qur'an, Surah 4: 34)*

Some Muslims believe that modern society is different and that due to improved employment opportunities and living costs, women now also have an important role in providing for the family.

The Prophet Muhammad is called 'an excellent model' (Surah 33: 21). Muslims look up to him as the best example of how to live their life, including in the home. The Prophet himself performed many household chores, including mending his own clothes. This shows that men also have a domestic role in the home:

> ❝ When asked what the Prophet did in the house, his wife 'A'ishah said: "He used to work for his family, and when prayer [time] came, he went out for prayer". ❞
>
> *(Hadith – Sahih Al-Bukhari)*

 A A Muslim husband is responsible for taking good care of his wife: 'The best of you are those who are best towards their wives' (Hadith – Tirmidhi)

What might Muslim men learn from this Hadith? **STRETCH**

The role of women

Many Muslims believe that the most important role for a woman is as a wife and mother, as this is part of her nature given by Allah:

> ❛"Our Lord is He who gave everything its form, then gave it guidance."❜
> *(Qur'an, Surah 20: 50)*

The Qur'an teaches that women should marry and remain faithful to their husbands:

> ❛Righteous wives are devout and guard what God would have them guard in their husbands' absence.❜
> *(Qur'an, Surah 4: 34)*

B Muslim women have the right to work and earn for themselves

Traditionally, women are expected to run the home, teach Islam to their children, and train them to become good Muslims. This is because they are likely to spend the most time with them. However, the husband must also give his full support.

Wives have the right to work, but are not required to give any part of their earnings to men. The Qur'an teaches that women can own property and inherit wealth (see 2.8). These rights are denied in some patriarchal Muslim societies because of culture. A patriarchal society is one in which men hold most or all of the power and influence.

The role of men and women in the family in the time of Muhammad

Muslims believe that in the time of the Prophet Muhammad, humanity was in need of divine guidance as society had become corrupt and had moved away from God. Womanizing and incest (sex between two close relatives, for example a brother and sister) were common in Arabia, and women were treated as inferior. The practice of female infanticide (killing baby girls due to the shame they brought to poor families) was also a custom among some Arabs.

Muslims believe Allah chose Muhammad to teach people that this was wrong and that women needed to be valued and respected. The Prophet's own wives have been called mothers of the believers (Surah 33: 6), and his youngest wife, 'A'ishah, was one of the first scholars of Islam and teachers of Muslims. These point to the high spiritual and social status that women enjoyed when Muhammad brought Islam.

When the Qur'an was revealed, men and women were both required to make an active contribution to creating a more moral society, as this is the aim of Islam:

> ❛The believers, both men and women, support each other; they order what is right and forbid what is wrong❜
> *(Qur'an, Surah 9: 71)*

Today, Muslim men and women are equally responsible for making sure that they:

- show 'love and kindness' towards each other
  (Surah 30: 21)
- promote an Islamic environment in their home
- teach their children Muslim etiquette.

Equality

- Most Muslims believe that men and women have clearly defined roles that are natural to them and part of Allah's plan.
- Having different responsibilities does not mean men and women are unequal.
- Some Muslims argue that greater rights and opportunities for women today mean that traditional views about the roles of men and women need to be redefined in the twenty-first century.

 CASE STUDY: KYMBERLEY

I believe men and women are completely equal within the family but that equality doesn't mean they have to do the same job as each other. However, nobody should be expected to perform a certain task because of their gender, apart from giving birth of course – women are probably stuck with that one! There are things that have to happen as part of family life for it to function effectively and it doesn't matter whether the person who does that job is male or female as long as they get it done.
(Kymberley, cheerleader)

Would Muslims agree with **SUPPORT** Kymberley? Be ready to share your view in class.

 BUILD YOUR SKILLS

1   Describe one Muslim belief about the role of men and one about the role of women in the family. **SUPPORT**

2   Describe how the roles of men and women have changed since the time of Muhammad.

3   Do you think the roles of men and women in the home are equal? Discuss your views with a partner.

 SUMMARY

- Islam teaches that men and women are different but equal.
- The roles of men and women are defined according to the teachings of the Qur'an and the Hadith.
- Men and women have similar but also different roles in the family.

 EXAM-STYLE QUESTIONS

a   Outline **three** beliefs about the roles of men and women in the family. (3)

d   'There is no equality in Islam.' Evaluate this statement considering arguments for and against. In your response you should:
- refer to Muslim teachings
- refer to different Muslim points of view
- reach a justified conclusion. (12)

2.8 Gender prejudice and discrimination

Did you know that even as recently as the early twentieth century, women in the UK:

- who got divorced were shunned by society and treated as outcasts?
- could not vote?
- were not able to graduate from the country's top universities?

How do Muslim teachings oppose gender prejudice and discrimination?

In Islam, men and women are spiritually equal and judged in the same way before Allah:

> ❝To whoever, male or female, does good deeds and has faith, We shall give a good life and reward them according to the best of their actions.❞
> *(Qur'an, Surah 16: 97)*

> ❝For men and women who are devoted to God [...] God has prepared forgiveness and a rich reward.❞
> *(Qur'an, Surah 33: 35)*

These verses emphasize how both men and women who have faith and act according to the teachings of Islam have an equal reward. Muslims use these and other teachings to argue that all **gender prejudice** and **gender discrimination** is wrong.

SPECIFICATION FOCUS

Muslim teaching about gender prejudice and discrimination: Muslim attitudes to gender prejudice and discrimination, including Surah 33: 35; examples of gender equality in action in Islam

USEFUL TERMS

Gender prejudice: believing that one gender is less or more important than another

Gender discrimination: treating people less or more favourably because of their gender

Now-days when women talk about Automatic Washing

...they talk about *Wonderful Whirlpool*

A An advert from the 1950s – does this show gender prejudice?

No ill treatment or discrimination are allowed with respect to things like marriage and inheritance:

> 'You who believe, it is not lawful for you to … treat your wives harshly'
> *(Qur'an, Surah 4: 19)*

> 'Men shall have a share in what their parents and closest relatives leave, and women shall have a share in what their parents and closest relatives leave'
> *(Qur'an, Surah 4: 7)*

Copy out one teaching and explain how it shows Muslim opposition to gender prejudice and discrimination.

STRETCH

B The Qur'an teaches that men and women are spiritually equal

CASE STUDY: YVONNE

A careful reading of the Qur'an shows that just about everything that Western feminists fought for in the 1970s was available to Muslim women 1,400 years ago. Women in Islam are considered equal to men in spirituality, education and worth, and a woman's gift for childbirth and child-rearing is regarded as a positive attribute.
(Yvonne Ridley, 'How I came to love the veil', The Washington Post, 22 October 2006)

What teachings might have led Yvonne Ridley to convert to Islam? Write no more than 100 words.

SUPPORT

Yvonne Ridley, a journalist, was kidnapped by the Taliban in Afghanistan and was released on the condition that she read the Qur'an when she returned to Britain. She kept her word, and after reading it decided to become a Muslim

How can gender equality be seen in action in Islam?

There are many Muslims who believe that women cannot be religious leaders because the prophets and khalifahs have always been men. Others argue that in Islamic history, both past and present, Muslims have been led by women in religion, politics and war.

Muslims argue that society is now less patriarchal (dominated by men). Better access to education and employment opportunities have led to changing attitudes about the role of women. A number of women have risen to political power in Muslim-majority countries, such as Benazir Bhutto (Pakistan), Megawati Sukarnoputri (Indonesia), Khaleda Zia (Bangladesh) and Masoumeh Ebtekar (Iran). These countries have the world's largest Muslim populations. Some Muslims therefore ask: why can't women become leaders in Islam too?

An increasing number of women are now involved in the management of mosques. In Islam, women are allowed to lead other women in prayer, but traditionally women have not led men in this way. In 2008, the Muslim Educational Centre of Oxford created controversy when it invited a female scholar, Amina Wadud, to lead both men and women in Salah:

> ❝ There is nothing in the Qur'an that prohibits it. My own theological research into the essence of Islam indicates the necessity for us to be able to move away from the tradition that restricted women from the practice of leading prayer. ❞
> *(Amina Wadud)*

> ❝ We have no objections to women being heads of state, or organisation leaders. Women are highly respected in Islam. But in Islamic law, women cannot lead prayer. ❞
> *(Maryan Ramzy)*

Do you agree with Amina or Maryan? Explain why. STRETCH How do you think the other would respond to your views? Refer to Islamic teachings and beliefs in your answer.

> ❝ There are women fighting the feminist fight within religion [...] their work is important, as they strive to change a tradition that has no space for them. They're demanding the right to reinterpret their religion. ❞
> *(Mona Eltahawy, journalist)*

Most Muslims argue that fifteen centuries of theological scholarship and research has recorded that it is always men who lead mixed prayers and this is in no way discriminatory towards women. They say equality is not 'sameness' but in each gender being able to freely play their part in all walks of life.

SCHOLARS ENDORSE STATEMENT ON THE FULL INCLUSION OF WOMEN IN MOSQUES

We, the undersigned Muslim scholars, leaders, organizations and concerned Muslims, voice our strong commitment to uphold and realize the Prophetic ideal of masjids being open and inclusive of women. Striving to realize the Prophetic model, we call upon all masjids to ensure that (1) women are welcomed as an integral part of masjids and encouraged to attend, (2) women have a prayer space in the main *musalla* which is behind the lines of men but not behind a full barrier that disconnects women from the main *musalla* and prevents them from seeing the imam; and (3) women actively participate in the decision-making process of the masjid, best realized by having women on the governing bodies of masjids.

LIKE US ON FACEBOOK

Imams Online
199,773 likes

Like Page   Watch Video

 The website imamsonline. com published a statement calling for greater inclusion of women in mosques

Most Muslims feel that gender prejudice and discrimination are wrong and against the teachings of the Qur'an and the Hadith. Women have always had a high status in Islam and played an important role in the early days and spread of the ummah. Although there is nothing to stop a Muslim woman pursuing a career, her primary responsibility is to her family as this is part of the nature Allah has given her (see 2.7). Many Muslim women are able to balance their jobs with their commitments to their husband and children.

BUILD YOUR SKILLS

1 Explain what gender prejudice and gender discrimination are, and why Muslims believe they are wrong.

2 Can you think of roles that will always seem to be more for men than women, and for women more than men? Does this necessarily mean men and women are unequal? Explain your answer. **STRETCH**

SUMMARY

- Attitudes towards gender roles have changed a lot in society, especially in the last 100 years.

- These changes have come about through changes in law that have allowed women to be treated equally, although many argue there is still a long way to go.

- Islam teaches that men and women are spiritually equal and that many rights given to Western women recently were already granted to Muslim women at the time of Muhammad.

? EXAM-STYLE QUESTIONS

b Explain **two** ways that gender discrimination might occur. (4)

d 'If more people followed Muslim teachings, there would be less gender prejudice.'
Evaluate this statement considering arguments for and against. In your response you should:
- refer to Muslim teachings
- refer to different Muslim points of view
- reach a justified conclusion. (12)

Revision

BUILD YOUR SKILLS

Look at the list of 'I can' statements below and think carefully about how confident you are. Use the following code to rate each of the statements. Be honest!

Green – very confident. What is your evidence for this?

Orange – quite confident. What is your target? Be specific.

Red – not confident. What is your target? Be specific.

A self-assessment revision checklist is available on *Kerboodle*

I can...

- Explain the significance of marriage in Muslim life, including reference to Surah 4: 1–24 and Surah 24: 30–34

- Explain non-religious (including atheist and Humanist) attitudes to the importance of marriage in society, including it not being important and cohabitation

- Explain Muslim responses to non-religious attitudes to the importance of marriage

- Explain Muslim teachings on sexual relationships outside of marriage, including reference to Surah 23: 5–11 and homosexuality

- Explain non-religious (including atheist and Humanist) attitudes to sexual relationships, including the acceptance of sex outside marriage and homosexuality

- Explain Muslim responses to non-religious attitudes to sexual relationships

- Explain Muslim teachings about the purpose and importance of families, including reference to Surah 46: 15–18, procreation and the strengthening of the ummah

- Give divergent Muslim responses to the different types of family within 21st-century society, including nuclear, single parent, same-sex parents, extended and blended families

- Describe how the Muslim community supports families, including through worship, rites of passage, classes for parents and children, and counselling

- Explain why the Muslim community tries to support families

- Give divergent understandings of the importance of this support for Muslims today and how it might strengthen the ummah, with reference to Surah 3: 102–105

- Give divergent Muslim teachings and attitudes about contraception and family planning, including reference to Sahih Al-Bukhari 34: 432 and 62: 136

- Explain different non-religious (including atheist and Humanist) attitudes to family planning

- Explain how ethical theories such as situation ethics can be applied to family planning

- Explain Muslim responses to non-religious attitudes to family planning and the application of ethical theories, such as situation ethics, to family planning

- Explain divergent Muslim beliefs, teachings and attitudes towards divorce and remarriage, including reference to Surah 2: 226–241

- Give the different rules for performing a divorce in Shi'a and Sunni Islam

- Explain different non-religious (including atheist and Humanist) attitudes to divorce and remarriage

- Explain how ethical theories, such as situation ethics, can be applied to divorce and remarriage

- Explain Muslim responses to non-religious attitudes to divorce and remarriage and the application of ethical theories, such as situation ethics, to divorce and remarriage

- Give divergent Muslim beliefs, teachings and attitudes about the role of men and women in the family, with reference to the Qur'an, including Surah 4, and the time of Muhammad

- Explain Muslim attitudes to gender prejudice and discrimination, including reference to Surah 33: 35

- Give examples of gender equality in action in Islam

Exam practice

On these exam practice pages you will see example answers for each of the exam question types: **a**, **b**, **c** and **d**. You can find out more about these on pages 6–11.

• Question 'a'

*Question **a** is AO1 – it tests your knowledge and understanding.*

> (a) Outline **three** Muslim teachings about family. (3)

Student response

Muslims teach that family is important, respecting parents is good, and that living single is OK.

Improved student response

Muslims believe that family is the foundation of society. Islam teaches that the mother has a very important role to play, and for this reason 'paradise lies at the feet' of your mothers (Hadith – Nasa'i). Family is also important so that children can be brought up according to the teachings of the Qur'an.

 Over to you! Give yourself three minutes on the clock and have a go at answering this question.

 WHAT WENT WELL

This is a low level answer. The student has understood the requirement to provide three points. 'Respecting parents' may be credited.

 HOW TO IMPROVE

'Family is important' is not a Muslim teaching. 'Living single is OK' is not correct. This student clearly needs to revise this area more.

• Question 'b'

*Question **b** is AO1 – it tests your knowledge and understanding.*

> (b) Explain **two** reasons why there are different Muslim attitudes to contraception. (4)

Student response

Muslim attitudes to contraception are different because using protection like condoms is a personal choice and religion cannot stop you from doing what you want.

Improved student response

There is very little direct teaching about contraception in the Qur'an or the Hadith, which is why Muslims have different attitudes to it and do not always agree with each other about whether contraception is acceptable. If there was more specific guidance about contraception in the shari'ah, Muslims would not be divided, so this is one explanation for why they have different views.

Another reason for differences is because of how particular Muslim teachings are interpreted. Children are a gift from Allah, therefore many Muslims would say that anything that obstructs or interferes with this – such as contraception – is wrong. However, others emphasize that the Prophet Muhammad knew of his

 WHAT WENT WELL

This is a low level answer that contains nothing worthy of credit.

 HOW TO IMPROVE

Answers should reflect that people who are religious are believers for a reason and often put their faith ahead of personal choice. The question acknowledges that there are different Muslim attitudes about contraception and the answer needs to explain why these differences exist – as has been done in the improved student response. It is helpful to separate the first explanation from the second. A simple way of doing this is to start the second paragraph with 'Another reason...'

followers using the withdrawal method and did not say this was wrong, so some Muslims say this is OK.

 Over to you! Give yourself four minutes on the clock and have a go at answering this question.

• Question 'c'

*Question **c** is AO1 – it tests your knowledge and understanding.*

> (c) Explain **two** reasons why Muslim teachings about sexual relationships are relevant today. In your answer you must refer to a source of wisdom and authority. (5)

Student response

There are lots of teachings in the Qur'an and the Hadith about sex. For Muslims, sex is only allowed within marriage, therefore any act of physical love outside of this is haram. It is so serious that the Qur'an says that the punishment is death, and this is what we see in many Muslim countries. I think this is too strict as there are many couples that want to see if they can live with each other first, before taking the step of marrying.

Improved student response

There are lots of teachings in the Qur'an and the Hadith about sex which Muslims believe are still relevant. Although attitudes in society have changed a lot and there are more people now choosing to cohabit, or even live in same-sex relationships, most Muslims would be against these. One of the reasons Islam forbids homosexuality (story of Lot in the Qur'an, Surah 7) is because it does not enable a couple to have children, and therefore goes against one of the purposes of our creation.

Additionally, Muslims would argue that marriage is more likely to prevent people from having casual sexual relationships, which often lead to unhappiness and even sexually transmitted infections. The Qur'an refers to such relationships as 'obscene' (Qur'an, Surah 6: 151) as they can be unhealthy for society. Therefore Muslims consider these teachings to still be very relevant today.

 Over to you! Give yourself five minutes on the clock and have a go at answering this question.

• Question 'd'

*Question **d** is both AO1 and AO2 – this tests your knowledge and understanding as well as your ability to evaluate.*

> (d) 'There is no such thing as a "normal" type of family.'
> Evaluate this statement, considering arguments for and against. In your response you should:
> • refer to Muslim teachings
> • refer to non-religious views
> • reach a justified conclusion (12)

✓ **WHAT WENT WELL**

This is a low level answer. 'Sex is only allowed within marriage' is accurate and there is good use of a key word (haram).

! **HOW TO IMPROVE**

It is important not to misrepresent teachings. While sex outside of marriage is condemned by the Qur'an, it does not sanction death as the punishment. Muslim countries are often seen as bad examples of Islamic teachings. Therefore a good answer will include at least one specific teaching as evidence, as the improved student response demonstrates.

It is also important to read the question properly so that you don't miss important commands, such as the instruction to include a reference to a source of wisdom and authority. There is no requirement for a personal opinion in this question either.

Student response

I agree that there is no such thing as a 'normal' type of family as attitudes to family life have changed so much, especially in the last few decades. For instance, the 'normal' type of family in the 1950s was a traditional family made up of a husband, wife and children who were born in the marriage. However, now almost half of children are born outside of marriage. This is because a lot more couples are choosing to cohabit and don't feel the need for a wedding to show their love for each other. Same-sex marriages are also legal now, which wasn't the case until very recently. However, others would say that the nuclear family remains the most common type, and Muslims would say that this is the only acceptable type too, where a man and woman marry, and then have children. This type of family is at the heart of Islam. The Qur'an clearly sets out roles for both men and women in a family. Muslims see this as the most stable type of family as this is how children are brought up in the faith, which then shapes them for the rest of their lives.

Improved student response

I agree that there is no such thing as a 'normal' type of family as attitudes to family life have changed so much, especially in the last few decades. For instance, the 'normal' type of family in the 1950s was a traditional family made up of a husband, wife and children who were born in the marriage. This is known as the nuclear family. However, now almost half of children are born outside of marriage. This is because many more couples are choosing to cohabit and don't feel the need for a wedding to show their love for each other. Same-sex marriages are also legal now which wasn't the case until very recently. Many in society see this as a very positive thing. Therefore trends have changed quite significantly.

However, others argue that the nuclear family – where a man and woman marry, and then have children – remains the most common type of family. This type of family lies at the heart of Islam. The Qur'an says Allah, 'created spouses from among yourselves for you to live in tranquillity: He ordained love and kindness between you.' (Qur'an, Surah 30: 21). This means that the only family type Allah accepts is the one in which a man and woman are joined in marriage. This is also how the Prophet Muhammad lived his life, and Muslims must strive to follow his example. Islam also clearly sets out roles for both men and women in a family. For instance, men are given the responsibility of earning a living so that they can provide for their families, while women have the primary role of bringing up their children. Muslims see this as the most stable type of family, because this is how children are brought up in the faith, which then shapes them for the rest of their lives. They believe this would be lacking in other types of family where the absence of one parent or parents of opposite genders would have an adverse impact on a child's upbringing. However, there are some single-parent Muslims who have had a poor experience of married life and do not feel the need for a partner to help them bring up their children.

In conclusion, I believe that with all the changes that have occurred in Britain in the last few years, family life has changed dramatically and so there isn't any one particular type that is 'normal'.

Over to you! Give yourself 12 minutes on the clock and have a go at answering this question.

✓ WHAT WENT WELL

This is a mid level answer. It is a balanced response, which reflects a good understanding of the changing nature of family life, UK laws and non-religious views.

! HOW TO IMPROVE

Knowledge of Islam at this level should be supported with evidence (e.g. quotes) with supporting explanations. The answer also requires a conclusion. Both are provided in the improved student response opposite.

✎ BUILD YOUR SKILLS

In your exams, you'll need to make sure you use religious terminology correctly. Do you know the meaning of the following important terms for this topic?

nikah   **ummah**   **adhan**

aqiqah   **shari'ah**   **khitan**

Chapter 3:
Living the Muslim Life

Chapter contents	Specification mapping	Page
Chapter 3: Living the Muslim Life	Section 3: Living the Muslim Life	75
3.1 Ten Obligatory Acts	3.1 Ten Obligatory Acts of Shi'a Islam: the nature, history and purpose of the Ten Obligatory Acts; the diversity of practice and importance of Ten Obligatory Acts for Shi'a Muslims today; their basis in the Qur'an, including reference to Surah 9: 71–73; divergent understandings of these principles within Sunni Islam, including links with the Five Pillars	77
3.2 Shahadah	3.2 Shahadah as one of the Five Pillars: the nature, role and significance of Shahadah for Sunni and Shi'a Muslims, including reference to Surah 3: 17–21; why reciting Shahadah is important for Muslims, and its place in Muslim practice today	79
3.3 Salah *This topic should be compared with Christianity.*	3.3 Salah as one of the Five Pillars, including reference to Surah 15: 98–99 and 29: 45: the nature, history, significance and purpose of Salah for Sunni and Shi'a Muslims, including different ways of understanding them; how Salah is performed including ablution, times, directions, movements and recitations, in the home and mosque and Jummah prayer	82
3.4 Sawm	3.4 Sawm as one of the Five Pillars: the nature, role, significance and purpose of fasting during Ramadan, including Surah 2: 183–185; those who are excused from fasting and why; the significance of the Night of Power: the nature, history and purpose of the Night of Power; why Laylat al-Qadr is important for Muslims today	85
3.5 Zakah and Khums	3.5 Zakah as one of the Five Pillars and Khums: the nature, role, significance and purpose of Zakah and Khums, including Surah 9: 58–60 and 8: 36–42; why Zakah is important for Sunni Muslims; why Khums is important for Shi'a Muslims; the benefits of receiving Zakah or Khums	89
3.6 Hajj	3.6 Hajj as one of the Five Pillars: the nature, role, origins and significance of Hajj, including Surah 2: 124–130; 22: 25–30; how Hajj is performed and why Hajj is important for Muslims; benefits and challenges from attending Hajj for Muslims	92
3.7 Jihad	3.7 Jihad: the origins, meaning and significance of jihad in Islam; divergent understandings of jihad within Islam, including the difference between lesser and greater jihad; the conditions for declaration of lesser jihad, including reference to Surah 2: 190–194 and 22: 39; the importance of jihad in the life of Muslims	95
3.8 Celebrations and Commemorations	3.8 The nature, origins, activities, meaning and significance of the celebration/commemoration of Id-ul-Adha, with reference to Surah 37: 77–111, and Id-ul-Fitr in Sunni Islam, with reference to their place within Shi'a Islam; and Id-ul-Ghadeer, with reference to Hadith and the interpretation of Surah 5: 3, and Ashura in Shi'a Islam, with reference to their place within Sunni Islam	98
Revision and Exam Practice	**Revision checklist, exam questions, sample answers and guidance**	**101**

3.1 Ten Obligatory Acts

SPECIFICATION FOCUS

Ten Obligatory Acts of Shi'a Islam: the nature, history and purpose of the Ten Obligatory Acts; the diversity of practice and importance of Ten Obligatory Acts for Shi'a Muslims today ; their basis in the Qur'an, including reference to Surah 9: 71–73; divergent understandings of these principles within Sunni Islam, including links with the Five Pillars

What are the Ten Obligatory Acts?

The **Ten Obligatory Acts** are the most important duties of a Shi'a Muslim. They are based on the Qur'an, the Hadith and the work of early Shi'a scholars. The table below describes each Act.

While it is Shi'a Muslims, and not Sunni Muslims, who use the phrase 'Ten Obligatory Acts', almost all of the Acts are also recognized and performed by Sunni Muslims.

The Ten Obligatory Acts are formulated by Shi'a scholars, but in reality Shi'a and Sunni Muslims share many of the same duties. For example, notice that the first four Acts are also four of the Five Pillars (see 3.2–3.6). However, Sunni Muslims do not give 20 per cent of their savings (Khums) (see 3.5).

	Act	Description	Teaching
1	Salah (see 3.3)	Praying five times a day	'keep up regular prayer, for prayer is obligatory for the believers at prescribed times.' *(Qur'an, Surah 4: 103)*
2	Sawm (see 3.4)	Fasting during the month of Ramadan	'You who believe, fasting is prescribed for you… so that you may be mindful of God.' *(Qur'an, Surah 2: 183)*
3	Hajj (see 3.6)	Pilgrimage to Makkah, Saudi Arabia	'Pilgrimage to the House is a duty owed to God by people who are able to undertake it.' *(Qur'an, Surah 3: 97)*
4	Zakah (see 3.5)	Alms to be given based on ownership of things like gold, cattle and crops	'whatever you give in charity, in your desire for God's approval, will earn multiple rewards.' *(Qur'an, Surah 30: 39)*
5	Khums (see 3.5)	Tax set at 20 per cent for causes decided by Shi'a leaders	'Know that one-fifth of your battle gains belongs to God and the Messenger, to close relatives and orphans, to the needy and travellers.' *(Qur'an, Surah 8: 41)*
6	Jihad (see 3.7)	Striving in the way of Allah	'You who believe, be mindful of God […] and strive for His cause, so that you may prosper.' *(Qur'an, Surah 5: 35)*
7	**Amr bil ma'roof**	Encouraging good actions	'The believers, both men and women, support each other; they order what is right.' *(Qur'an, Surah 9: 71)*
8	**Nahi anil munkar**	Discouraging evil actions	'The believers, both men and women, support each other; they […] forbid what is wrong.' *(Qur'an, Surah 9: 71)*
9	Tawalla	Association with good people, e.g. those who follow the ahl al-bayt	'Say [Prophet], "I ask no reward from you for this, only the affection due to kin".' *(Qur'an, Surah 42: 23)*
10	Tabarra	Disassociation with evil people	'You who believe, do not take My enemies and yours as your allies.' *(Qur'an, Surah 60: 1)*

How do Shi'a Muslims practise the Ten Obligatory Acts today?

Shi'a Muslims have a duty to fulfil each of these acts as well as they can. Some relate to individual actions, such as Salah and Sawm, while others are about ways of treating other people and behaving in society. For example, if a Shi'a Muslim sees a person in need, they should invite others to help too. This would be counted as Amr bil ma'roof. If a Shi'a Muslim sees a person smoking, drinking alcohol, or doing anything that might cause them or others harm, they should try to stop them. This would be an example of Nahi anil munkar.

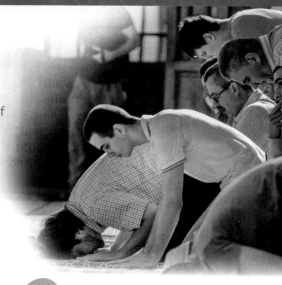

Why are the Ten Obligatory Acts important?

The Ten Obligatory Acts are crucial in guiding the practices of Shi'a Muslims. They are a way of showing commitment to Islam, not just through words, but deeds. Collectively they enable Shi'a Muslims to connect with Allah, purify their hearts, ease the suffering of the poor, and promote a better society. They are also a means for Shi'a Muslims to be blessed with a good afterlife:

> ‘God has promised the believers, both men and women, Gardens graced with flowing streams where they will remain ’
> (Qur'an, Surah 9: 72)

USEFUL TERMS

Amr bil ma'roof: encouraging good actions

Nahi anil munkar: discouraging evil actions

Ten Obligatory Acts: the most important duties of a Shi'a Muslim

 CASE STUDY: HASAN

Jews and Christians have the Ten Commandments and, in the same way, Shi'a Muslims have the Ten Obligatory Acts. "Obligatory" means they have to be done. Some are straightforward, like Salah, as this doesn't take too much time. Nahi anil munkar is often tricky as it's not always possible to get away from people who do bad things – like those who swear – but as long as I'm trying to be a positive influence, that's what's important.

 SUMMARY

- Shi'a Muslims believe in Ten Obligatory Acts based on the Qur'an, the Hadith and the work of early Shi'a scholars.

- These principles are important for Shi'a Muslims because they show commitment to their faith through action, not just words.

 BUILD YOUR SKILLS

1   Give yourself five minutes to look at the table on page 77. On your own or with a partner, close your books and write down as many of the Ten Obligatory Acts as you can remember. Then, check and correct your work.   **SUPPORT**

2   What do Hasan's comments say about the importance of following these principles for Shi'a Muslims?

3   Are any of the acts more important than the others? Write down your response with at least one reason.   **STRETCH**

 EXAM-STYLE QUESTIONS

a   State **three** of the Ten Obligatory Acts. (3)
b   Explain **two** ways that a Shi'a Muslim can show their commitment. (4)

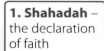
There are many important duties of a Muslim in Islam. These are drawn together in the **Five Pillars**, which come from the Qur'an and the Hadith. They have significance for both Shi'a and Sunni Muslims. They are:

1. Shahadah – the declaration of faith

3. Sawm – fasting during the month of Ramadan

5. Hajj – pilgrimage to Makkah, in Saudi Arabia

2. Salah – praying five times a day

4. Zakah – giving 2.5% of one's wealth to the poor every lunar year

 The Five Pillars

SPECIFICATION FOCUS

Shahadah as one of the Five Pillars: the nature, role and significance of Shahadah for Sunni and Shi'a Muslims, including reference to Surah 3: 17–21; why reciting Shahadah is important for Muslims, and its place in Muslim practice today

USEFUL TERMS

Five Pillars: the most important duties of a Muslim; also known as Arkaan al-Islam

Shahadah: declaration of belief, which Muslims are required to say

Shirk: a sin that involves setting up equals to Allah; worshipping anyone or anything besides him

You will be learning more about each of the Five Pillars in this chapter, starting with Shahadah.

What is the Shahadah and why is it significant?

Can you remember the last time you made a declaration or a firm commitment about something?

In addition to the many declarations or commitments Muslims may make, they make one very important declaration with both words and a firm belief in their hearts. This declaration is called the **Shahadah**.

The Shahadah is the first pillar and describes the essence of Islam. It consists of two key statements:

'I bear witness that there is none worthy of worship except Allah alone and He has no partner.

And I bear witness that Muhammad is His servant and His Messenger.'

For a number of Shi'a Muslims, the Shahadah also has a third part:

'And I bear witness that Ali is the Friend of God.'

The first part of the Shahadah relates to Tawhid (see 1.3), and the second to Risalah (see 1.4).

'There is no god except Allah' (Tawhid)

Muslims are required to believe that Allah is 'one' and without any partner. Muslims believe there is nothing worthy of worship except him. The Qur'an says:

> ❛God bears witness that there is no god but Him, as do the angels and those who have knowledge. [...] There is no god but Him, the Almighty, the All Wise. ❜
> *(Qur'an, Surah 3: 18–19)*

B The Shahadah in Arabic text

Muslims believe that worshipping or putting absolute trust in anything other than Allah is **shirk** because only he can give life, answer prayers, and provide for everyone's needs. In Islam, shirk is so serious that it is described as unforgivable:

> ❛**God does not forgive the joining of partners with Him**: anything less than that He forgives to whoever He will, but anyone who joins partners with God has fabricated a tremendous sin. ❜
> *(Qur'an, Surah 4: 48)*

The Prophet Muhammad lived at a time when people in Makkah practised idol worship and were known for having a different god for every day of the year. He preached against this and wanted people to believe in Tawhid.

'Muhammad is Allah's Servant and Messenger' (Risalah)

The second part of Shahadah requires belief in the Prophet Muhammad as a servant and messenger of Allah. Muslims believe this confirms Muhammad's humanity – he was a person just like everyone else. Being a servant means that his whole life was dedicated to serving Allah.

Muslims believe Muhammad was sent by Allah to deliver the final and universal message to the world. In the Qur'an, he is called 'an excellent model' (Surah 33: 41) and so Muslims look up to him as the best example of how to live.

Whenever Muslims recite the Shahadah, they are reminded of the core belief in Allah's oneness, and the importance of Muhammad as Allah's messenger.

> When using the name of the Prophet Muhammad, **SUPPORT** Muslims say 'peace and blessings of Allah be upon him' afterwards, and the shorter 'peace be upon him' after all other prophets and angels.

'Ali is the Friend of God'

Many Shi'a Muslims recite this final line because they believe that Ali was the rightful leader after Muhammad's death (see 1.1).

C Fans wait for their pop idol. Could this be an example of shirk? What do you think?

Why is the Shahadah important for Muslims?

- The Shahadah is the first pillar of Islam. It is a declaration of a Muslim's belief which has to come before all the other pillars. If anyone converts to Islam, these are the words they must recite. It is the basic requirement of faith.

- Shahadah is a testimony, which reminds a person about an important commitment they have made and will also make them more likely to honour it.

- Rewards are promised to those who put Allah and the Prophet before everything else:

> ❝Whoever obeys God and the Messenger will be among those He has blessed❞
> *(Qur'an, Surah 4: 69)*

What is the place of the Shahadah in Muslim practice today?

Muslims have recited the Shahadah since the time of the Prophet Muhammad. The Shahadah are the first words recited into the ears of a newborn child, repeated throughout a Muslim's life, and also during a person's burial. A person who repeats the Shahadah is called shahid (one who bears witness).

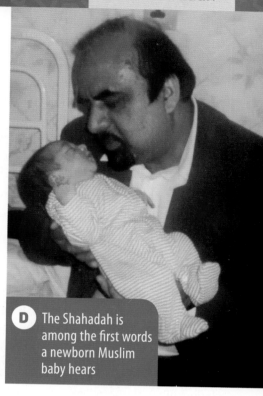

D The Shahadah is among the first words a newborn Muslim baby hears

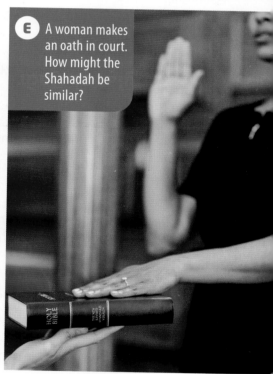

E A woman makes an oath in court. How might the Shahadah be similar?

BUILD YOUR SKILLS

1 Write down two important beliefs about the Shahadah.

SUPPORT

2 Explain why shirk is believed by Muslims to be a great sin.

3 'Shahadah is the most important pillar of Islam.' Do you agree with this statement? Explain your views.

STRETCH

SUMMARY

- Shahadah is the first pillar of Islam, recited by Sunni and Shi'a Muslims.

- Tawhid and Risalah are the two universal elements of the Shahadah.

- Shahadah is a testimony and commitment concerning a Muslim's faith.

EXAM-STYLE QUESTIONS

a Outline **three** beliefs about the Shahadah. (3)

c Explain **two** reasons why the Shahadah is important to Muslims. In your answer you must refer to a source of wisdom and authority. (5)

3.3 Salah

The Qur'an says that humans have been created to worship Allah. Anything that involves devotion for the sake of him is considered worship. The highest form of worship in Islam is **Salah**. Salah is a daily act of prayer. It is the second pillar of Islam.

> ❝Celebrate the glory of your Lord and be among those who bow down to Him: worship your Lord until what is certain comes to you.❞
> *(Qur'an, Surah 15: 98–99)*

What is the significance of Salah?

Muslims believe all prophets of Allah taught their followers about worship. Salah has existed since the time of the Prophet Muhammad, who demonstrated to Muslims how they should pray.

Muslims believe they can communicate directly with Allah, who desires a personal relationship with them. This is the greatest purpose of Salah, but there are others too. For example, Muslims can seek help in difficult times, and aim to improve themselves.

> ❝I respond to those who call Me, so let them respond to Me, and believe in Me, **so they may be guided**.❞
> *(Qur'an, Surah 2: 186)*

> ❝keep up the prayer: prayer restrains outrageous and unacceptable behaviour.❞
> *(Qur'an, Surah 29: 45)*

Salah is obligatory for all men and women. Children are also encouraged to develop the habit of praying from an early age. The Prophet Muhammad said that the first question Allah will ask Muslims on the Day of Judgement will be about Salah.

What is the nature of Salah?

Both Sunni and Shi'a Muslims offer five daily prayers, but there are some differences in how they are performed. For example, many Shi'a Muslims place a small block of earth, called turbah, on the ground as they believe that when they prostrate themselves their heads should touch something natural (e.g. wood). It is a reminder to them that just as they have come from the earth, they will return to it after death.

Ablution

Muslims believe there is a close link between the physical and spiritual. It is important to be clean before offering Salah, so Muslims perform ablution, or **wudu'**. This involves washing or wiping various parts of the face and body including hands, mouth, elbows and feet. Shi'a Muslims wipe the front of the head instead of the whole head as Sunni

SPECIFICATION FOCUS

Salah as one of the Five Pillars, including reference to Surah 15: 98–99 and 29: 45: the nature, history, significance and purpose of Salah for Sunni and Shi'a Muslims, including different ways of understanding them; how salah is performed including ablution, times, directions, movements and recitations, in the home and mosque and Jummah prayer

Copy out one of these verses and explain what you think it says about the purpose of Salah.   **SUPPORT**

'There is no link between the physical and spiritual.' **STRETCH** Write two paragraphs arguing for and against this statement. You must refer to Islam in your answer.

A A Muslim woman prepares for Salah by performing wudu'

Muslims do, and they wipe the top of the feet instead of washing them as Sunni Muslims do. Wudu' prepares worshippers physically and mentally for prayer.

Times

Salah should be offered at particular times in the day:

> ❝keep up regular prayer, for prayer is obligatory for the believers at prescribed times.❞
> *(Qur'an, Surah 4: 103)*

It is important for Muslims to try to observe each Salah on time, but work and other commitments can sometimes make this difficult. In these circumstances, some prayers, like Zuhr and Asr, can be combined. This is common among Shi'a Muslims, as they say that the Prophet Muhammad did the same.

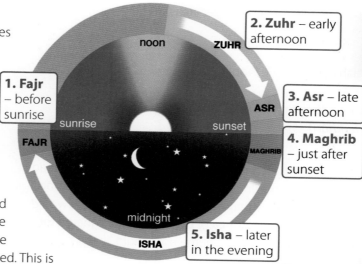

2. Zuhr – early afternoon

1. Fajr – before sunrise

3. Asr – late afternoon

4. Maghrib – just after sunset

5. Isha – later in the evening

B The five prayers and when they are performed

Direction

Salah must be performed facing Makkah, which is where the Ka'bah is located (see 3.6). The direction of prayer is called **qiblah**.

Movements

Each Salah is made up of a set sequence of actions and prayers, known as a **rak`ah**. There are different postures in each rak`ah, mainly:

- qiyam (standing)
- ruku` (bowing)
- sajdah (prostrating)
- qa`dah (kneeling).

C A worshipper in the sajdah position

Recitations

Salah must be offered in Arabic using set prayers taken from the Qur'an, Sunnah, and the Hadith. An example of a recitation that is repeated during Salah is the first chapter of the Qur'an.

Salah in the mosque

Although Salah can be offered anywhere, most Muslims pray in a mosque or at home. A mosque is dedicated to worshipping Allah. Prayers in a mosque create unity and strengthen the spiritual and social bond between Muslims. They are also believed to carry more blessings.

Mosques are houses of Allah so there are important rules that need to be followed by Muslims when they attend prayers. Some of the rules are:

- perform wudu', cover their heads, and remove their shoes beforehand
- switch off any devices like mobile phones to prevent possible disturbance
- enter calmly, say 'peace be upon you' as a greeting to those in the mosque, and then maintain silence before Salah starts.

◁|▷ **COMPARE AND CONTRAST**

Christianity is the main religious tradition of Great Britain. In your exam, you could be asked to **compare and contrast** the Salah, the daily act of prayer for Muslims, with Christian forms of worship. Create a table that explains the similarities and differences between them.

> ❝Prayer with the congregation is 27 times better than prayer performed by oneself❞
> *(Hadith – Sahih Al-Bukhari)*

Each Salah is preceded by the adhan to proclaim the start of the prayer. The Salah is led by an **Imam** in the mihrab (niche) which faces Makkah. Worshippers must keep straight rows and stand shoulder to shoulder. This symbolizes unity and equality. Men and women pray in separate prayer areas.

Salah at home

Many Muslims offer Salah at home. The Prophet Muhammad said:

> ❛Pray in your houses – do not make them like graveyards. ❜
> *(Hadith – Sahih Al-Bukhari)*

This means that homes should not become empty of spirituality, and encourages Muslims to offer some prayers at home. In some communities women do not attend Salah at the mosque and so only pray at home. At home Muslims would still perform wudu' and ensure that a clean area of the house is designated for Salah. Salah at home is usually led by the head of the household. It also trains children to pray regularly.

Jummah prayer

The most important day of the week for Muslims is Friday. This is when the **Jummah prayer** takes place in mosques. Jummah is a special weekly congregation that all Muslims try to attend. There are many blessings linked to the Jummah prayer as it is an opportunity for sins to be forgiven.

> ❛He who comes [...] to Jummah [...] offers the Salah and listens quietly when the Imam stands up for the sermon, **will have his sins forgiven** ❜
> *(Hadith, Sahih Al-Bukhari)*

USEFUL TERMS

Imam: person who leads Salah

Jummah prayer: a special congregation held every Friday, usually in the mosque

Qiblah: the direction Muslims face (towards Makkah) during Salah

Rak'ah: set of movements and words in each Salah

Salah: the Muslim prayer

Wudu': purification ritual to ensure one is clean before prayer

D The Jummah prayer brings Muslims together every week to listen to the Imam's sermon. Some are broadcast on Muslim TV channels

BUILD YOUR SKILLS

1   Create a revision mind-map on Salah. You should include why, how and where Muslims perform Salah.

2   Does it matter if Salah is offered alone or with others? Discuss with a partner.

3   Can prayer change anything? Write down a Muslim response, a non-religious response, and your own conclusions.   **STRETCH**

SUMMARY

- Muslims believe worship is the purpose of human creation.
- Salah is a daily act of prayer and is the second pillar of Islam.
- Salah is mostly performed in the mosque and sometimes at home or work.

EXAM-STYLE QUESTIONS

a   Outline **three** purposes of Salah. (3)

b   Describe **two** differences in worship between Islam and the main religious tradition of Great Britain. (4)

3.4 Sawm

Sawm is one of the five pillars of Islam. Sawm is the Arabic word for 'fasting'. There is one particular month, called **Ramadan**, when all Muslim men and women of good health must observe fasts.

In Islam, fasting involves giving up things for the sake of Allah. This includes food and drink for a number of hours every day, but also anything else that might lead to becoming distracted from remembering God – such as listening to pop music. Fasting starts from the first light of dawn and ends with sunset. Muslims believe it is important to eat something at both ends of the fast – breakfast at the start (suhur) and a dinner at the end (iftar). This was the practice of the Prophet Muhammad. The amount of food consumed should be moderate too. Ramadan is based on the lunar calendar, starting with the sighting of the new moon and ending with the Id-ul-Fitr festival (see 3.8). Ramadan is either 29 or 30 days long.

What is the significance of fasting during Ramadan?

This is an important passage about fasting during Ramadan:

> ❝You who believe, **fasting is prescribed for you**, as it was prescribed for those before you, so that you may be mindful of God [...] **It was in the month of Ramadan that the Qur'an was revealed** as guidance for mankind, clear messages giving guidance and distinguishing between right and wrong. [...] He [Allah] wants you to complete the prescribed period and to glorify Him for having guided you, **so that you may be thankful.**❞
> *(Qur'an, Surah 2: 183, 185)*

This mentions many important things about Sawm during Ramadan, including:

- It is 'prescribed', in other words, it is compulsory for all Muslims.
- This was the month that the angel Jibril first visited Muhammad to reveal the Qur'an, which Muslims consult on all matters of life.
- Fasting should bring Muslims closer to Allah and make them grateful for what they have.

During the fast, Muslims are supposed to spend more time in greater reflection of Allah's characteristics:

> ❝Whoever does not give up lying and evil deeds and saying bad words to others then God is not in need of their leaving food and drink.❞
> *(Hadith – Sahih Al-Bukhari)*

This means that Allah does not want people to fast if they do not become better people as a result.

A Sawm usually ends with the eating of dates, as was the practice of the Prophet Muhammad

What is the purpose of fasting in Ramadan?

There are several important reasons why Muslims fast during Ramadan:

- Muslims believe fasting will help them to get close to Allah. Extra prayers are offered in the night, which Muslims believe are granted special acceptance by Allah.
- Muslims believe that to experience hunger and thirst helps them to appreciate what some of the world's poorest people go through.
- Fasting can teach Muslims self-restraint and is a time to reflect on what they say and do, how they behave and treat others, and to try to change for the better. Being reminded of their own faults should make them overlook the weaknesses of others.
- Mosques are full of worshippers during this month, which brings the community much closer.
- Muslims believe fasting can help to make them purer, both spiritually and physically.

> Is it necessary to experience another person's hunger in order to understand it? Discuss with a partner. **STRETCH**

CASE STUDY: MUBARIZ

We all have to strive, and sometimes suffer, in order to attain a particular goal. The student who wants to excel at school, the professional who aspires to climb the career ladder, and the athlete who trains to become the best, must all struggle to accomplish their aims. No pain, no gain! Fasting works in the same way. Yes it can be difficult, but I feel like a much better person at the end of it. The rewards are definitely worth it.

Who is excused from fasting and why?

Some people are not required to fast. Based on Surah 2: 183–185 and the Hadith, these include:

- the sick
- travellers undertaking long journeys (e.g. flying abroad)
- the elderly
- those on medication
- pregnant and breastfeeding women
- young children.

Apart from children, Muslims who cannot keep the fast must either make up the missed days at another time, or pay fidyah, a monetary donation that puts food on the table for poor families.

According to the Qur'an, the reason for excusing these people from fasting is because Allah recognizes their 'extreme difficulty' and because 'God wants ease for you, not hardship' (Surah 2: 184–185).

> ❝Fast for a specific number of days, but if one of you is **ill**, or **on a journey**, then on other days later. For **those who can fast only with extreme difficulty**, there is a way to compensate – feed a needy person. But if anyone does good of his own accord, it is better for him, and fasting is better for you, if only you knew. ❞
> *(Qur'an, Surah 2: 184)*

What is the history of the Night of Power?

There is a link between Ramadan and an event that Muslims believe took place in the time of the Prophet Muhammad. This is when the angel Jibril visited Muhammad while he was praying in the cave Hira' (see image **B**). Jibril commanded him to read some words but Muhammad said he could not (as he had not been taught how to read and write). Jibril continued:

> ❛Read! In the name of your Lord who created: He created man from a clinging form. **Read! Your Lord is the Most Bountiful One** who taught by the pen, who taught man what he did not know. ❜
> *(Qur'an, Surah 96: 1–5)*

These were the first words revealed by Allah to Muhammad. This event is called **Laylat al-Qadr** (Night of Power) and took place in the month of Ramadan. This was the start of his prophethood.

What is the nature of the Night of Power?

Muslims believe that like the Prophet Muhammad, they can also experience their own Laylat al-Qadr. This is especially during the month of Ramadan. Muslim scholars have explained the nature of Laylat al-Qadr in different ways. Some have understood it to be a particular night when a person has all their prayers accepted, others interpret it to be a moment when angels come to the support of someone or a particular matter.

> ❛The Night of Glory is better than a thousand months; on that night the angels and the Spirit [Jibril] descend again and again with their Lord's permission on every task. ❜
> *(Qur'an, Surah 97: 3–4)*

This Surah refers to the Night of Power being better than a thousand months. Muslims believe this means that no one can measure the extent of its greatness and rewards.

SUPPORT Muslims believe that, because Allah created human beings, he is able to teach them things they might think they are unable to do – such as to read.

B Cave Hira', where the Prophet Muhammad experienced the Night of Power

What is the purpose of the Night of Power?

- Laylat al-Qadr was the start of the revelation of the Qur'an, which Muslims believe to be the final message from Allah to humanity.
- It was the time Muhammad was called to become a prophet for the whole of humanity.
- Muslims can also experience their own Laylat al-Qadr as a way of strengthening their faith in Islam and becoming closer to Allah.

Why is Laylat al-Qadr important for Muslims today?

- Laylat al-Qadr has a special significance especially in Ramadan when Muslims seek to become closer to God and to become blessed. The last few nights of the month provide them with an opportunity to achieve a high level of devotion. This is why some Muslims spend the final days of Ramadan in i`tikaf, in seclusion to focus on prayer, reflection, and repentance.
- Muhammad advised his followers to seek Laylat al-Qadr on one of the odd nights towards the end of the fasting month – specifically the twenty-first, twenty-third, twenty-fifth, twenty-seventh, or twenty-ninth nights. This is one of the reasons mosques are full in the evenings during Ramadan.
- Muslims believe that Laylat al-Qadr can remove past sins.

 C Mosques are full in the last ten days of Ramadan as Muslims try to experience Laylat al-Qadr

D Some Muslims spend the final days of Ramadan in i'tikaf, during which they have a private space allocated within the mosque to study, worship, and rest

 BUILD YOUR SKILLS

1. Create a revision mind-map about fasting, including how and when Muslims fast, why Muslims fast, and the Night of Power for Muhammad and for Muslims today.

2. Would a benevolent God require people to fast in order to get close to him? Discuss in pairs and then write down:
   a. what an non-religious person would argue
   b. what a Muslim would argue
   c. your opinion.

3. Identify at least two ways that Laylat al-Qadr for Muhammad and for Muslims is **a** similar and **b** different. **STRETCH**

 SUMMARY

- Sawm is one of the pillars of Islam. All healthy Muslims, male and female, are required to fast during Ramadan.
- The primary aim of fasting is to become closer to Allah.
- The Night of Power was experienced by the Prophet Muhammad when he received the first of many revelations from Allah.
- Muslims also seek Laylat al-Qadr during the last ten days of Ramadan as a way of developing a closer relationship with Allah.

? **EXAM-STYLE QUESTIONS**

a. Explain **two** ways that Muslims observe Ramadan. (4)

d. 'Fasting should be an individual choice, not compulsory.'
Evaluate this statement considering arguments for and against. In your response you should:
- refer to Muslim teachings
- reach a justified conclusion. (15)

Do you want to become rich? What would you spend your money on? Should any of it be given to the poor?

Muslims believe that wealth is both a blessing from Allah and entrusted to people by him to be used responsibly. There are some types of charity in Islam which are optional, known as **sadaqah**, and can be any amount. Others are compulsory and are set at a fixed rate or percentage.

Both Sunni and Shi'a Muslims believe they have a duty to allocate part of the value of their earnings and belongings to those in need. While they have similar beliefs regarding this, there are also some differences.

> ❝Alms [food or money given to the poor] are meant only for the poor, the needy, those who administer them, those whose hearts need winning over, to free slaves and help those in debt, for God's cause, and for travellers in need.❞
> *(Qur'an, Surah 9: 60)*

What is Zakah?

Zakah is a pillar of Islam and is compulsory for all Muslims. Both Sunni and Shi'a Muslims believe in this. Zakah literally means 'purification'. This means that observing Zakah allows the money that people earn to become a source of goodness, or 'pure', for both the individual and the community.

Zakah is a system of social welfare that has existed since the time of the Prophet Muhammad. Muslims pay a contribution of 2.5 per cent of their wealth. This includes gold, silver and individual savings above a certain amount at the end of each lunar year. This ensures the heart of the person paying Zakah is purified from any selfishness and greed and their remaining wealth is purified and blessed.

Zakah is only given by Muslims who meet a certain threshold or minimum amount of wealth, known as **nisab**. This applies once they have met their own basic needs and those of their families. There are two measures to determine nisab: gold and silver.

- Gold: The nisab for gold is between 85 and 87 grams (approx.) depending on the various schools of Islamic law.
- Silver: The nisab for silver is between 59 and 63 grams (approx.) depending on the various schools of Islamic law.

SPECIFICATION FOCUS

Zakah as one of the Five Pillars and Khums: the nature, role, significance and purpose of Zakah and Khums, including Surah 9: 58–60 and 8: 36–42; why Zakah is important for Sunni Muslims; why Khums is important for Shi'a Muslims; the benefits of receiving Zakah or Khums

USEFUL TERMS

Khums: a system for Shi'a Muslims to pay an additional 20 per cent of their savings towards community causes

Nisab: the amount of wealth above which a Muslim needs to pay Zakah

Sadaqah: voluntary charity, not fixed at any rate

Zakah: literally 'purification' (of wealth), one of the pillars of Islam

To give an example, at the end of a year a Muslim might have 100 grams of gold. The Muslim would keep hold of around 87 grams (because this is the nisab), and have 13 grams left over. They would give 2.5 per cent of this remaining amount as Zakah.

SUPPORT

A Zakah is payable on jewellery that is above the nisab

Zakah is given to the state in a Muslim country, and to mosques in other countries like the UK, who must make sure that the wealth is distributed to the people that need it. The identity of everyone is meant to be kept confidential – neither the givers nor the receivers should be aware of whom the money has been given by and to.

Why do you think those giving and receiving Zakah are kept anonymous? **STRETCH**

Zakah can be used for any of the following:

- relieving poverty and distress
- helping those in debt
- providing comfort and convenience for travellers
- providing ransom for prisoners of war
- other things beneficial for society.

Why is Zakah important for Muslims?

- One of the meanings of Islam is 'peace', so it is important for Muslims to create a harmonious society that does not forget the less fortunate.
- Muslims believe Zakah is a form of worship – in the Qur'an, it is usually linked to Salah, like in the following verse: '[People], keep up the prayer, pay the prescribed alms [Zakah], and obey the Messenger, so that you may be given mercy' (Surah 24: 56).

Why is Zakah believed to be an act of worship? **STRETCH**

- All acts of charity will be rewarded, like a loan which will be repaid by Allah: 'pay the prescribed alms, and lend God a good loan. Whatever you store up for yourselves you will find with God, better and with a greater reward' (Surah 73: 20).
- Those who pay Zakah are counted among the successful believers (Surah 23: 4).
- Failure to use wealth in the right way can lead to serious consequences: 'They [disbelievers] use their wealth to bar people from the path of God, and they will go on doing so. In the end this will be a source of intense regret for them: they will be overcome and herded towards Hell' (Surah 8: 36).

What is Khums?

In addition to Zakah, Shi'a Muslims believe that 20 per cent of one's wealth should be given towards other causes too. This is based on the Qur'an:

> ❝ Know that **one-fifth of your battle gains belongs to God and the Messenger,** to close relatives and orphans, to the needy and travellers ❞
> (Qur'an, Surah 8: 41)

The scope of this verse for Sunni Muslims is limited to 'battle gains', while for Shi'a Muslims it is much wider than that. After the Prophet Muhammad's death, Shi'a Muslims would have given one fifth of their savings every year to the Imam of the time, who would spend it in whatever way he considered necessary for the Muslim community.

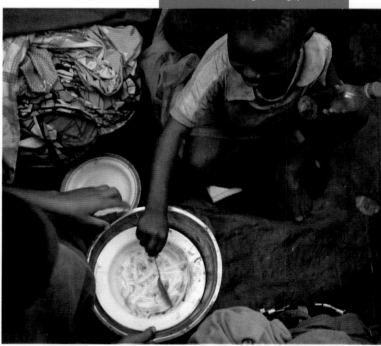

B Through Zakah, in an Islamic society, the poor are not allowed to go hungry

The Imam for Twelver Shi'a Muslims today – who is the twelfth and final Imam after Imam Ali – is not accessible as it is believed that Allah is keeping him until it is the right time to send him. In the meanwhile, Twelver Shi'a Muslims give **Khums** to their leader, the Grand Ayatollah, who then spends the money on orphanages, schools, mosques, and any other religious cause.

Why is Khums important to Shi'a Muslims?

- Serving others is part of the faith. The Prophet Muhammad said that 'the upper hand is better than the lower hand' *(Hadith)*, meaning it is more important to give than to receive.

- Like Zakah, Khums must be paid annually. Shi'a Muslims believe that failure to do so would mean that any money owned is not pure.

What are the benefits of receiving Zakah and Khums?

Receiving Zakah and Khums can improve the quality of life for the less fortunate in society.

Khums can also benefit people in a number of ways, including:

- better access to education when Khums is used to build learning centres
- helping to spread the Shi'a tradition, such as through publishing books.

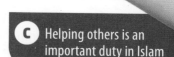

C Helping others is an important duty in Islam

 BUILD YOUR SKILLS

1   Copy and complete the following table:

	What is it (how much is given, etc.)?	Who gives it?	Who receives it?	Why is it given?
Zakah				
Khums				

2   Why are all Muslims taught to give the same percentage rather than the same amount? Discuss with a partner.

3   'People should give money to charity out of their free will, not because a holy book says so.' Do you agree with this non-religious view? Give reasons.

SUMMARY

- Zakah is one of the pillars of Islam. All Muslims must give 2.5 per cent of their annual savings if they meet the nisab.

- Shi'a Muslims also pay Khums, fixed at 20 per cent, towards community causes.

? **EXAM-STYLE QUESTIONS**

b   Explain **two** reasons why Muslims give to the poor. (4)

d   'It's the duty of governments, not individuals, to take care of the less fortunate.'
Evaluate this statement considering arguments for and against. In your response you should:
- refer to Muslim teachings
- reach a justified conclusion. (15)

3.6 Hajj

Makkah is a city in Saudi Arabia. For Muslims it is the holiest place on earth and is where prophets like Ibrahim, Isma'il, and Muhammad lived and preached. The **Ka'bah** there is believed by Muslims to be the first place in the world that was dedicated to the worship of Allah. For this reason, Makkah is a natural place of **pilgrimage** for Muslims. This pilgrimage is called **Hajj**, and is one of the Five Pillars of Islam.

Muslims who are physically able and can afford all the expenses to complete it at least once in their lives must perform Hajj (Surah 3: 97). There must also be a safe route to Makkah.

The time of Hajj is based on the lunar calendar, and ends in the festival of Id-ul-Adha (see 3.8). The pilgrimage starts on the eighth day of the month Dhu al-Hijjah and lasts about five days.

What are the origins of Hajj?

The origins of Hajj can be traced back around 4000 years to the time of Ibrahim (see 1.4). According to the Qur'an, Ibrahim was chosen by Allah to be a 'leader of people' (Surah 2: 124). The following story describes how Allah established the Ka'bah through Ibrahim:

> ❝We made the House [Ka'bah] a resort and a sanctuary for people, saying, "Take the spot where Abraham [Ibrahim] stood as your place of prayer." We commanded Abraham and Ishmael: **"Purify My House for those who walk round it, those who stay there, and those who bow and prostrate themselves in worship."** Abraham said, "My Lord, make this land secure and provide with produce those of its people who believe in God and the Last Day." God said, "As for those who disbelieve, I will grant them enjoyment for a short while and then subject them to the torment of the Fire – an evil destination."
>
> As Abraham and Ishmael **built up the foundations of the House** [they prayed], "Our Lord, accept [this] from us. You are the All Hearing, the All Knowing."❞
> *(Qur'an, Surah 2: 125–127)*

SPECIFICATION FOCUS

Hajj as one of the Five Pillars: the nature, role, origins and significance of Hajj, including Surah 2: 124–130; 22: 25–30; how Hajj is performed and why Hajj is important for Muslims; benefits and challenges from attending Hajj for Muslims

USEFUL TERMS

Hajj: the pilgrimage made by Muslims to Makkah

Ka'bah: cube-shaped building in Makkah which Muslims believe was the first house of Allah on earth, rebuilt by Ibrahim and Isma'il

Pilgrimage: a journey to a place which is special for religious reasons

Tawaf: anti-clockwise circuit of the Ka'bah, completed seven times during Hajj

This quotation from the Qur'an says the following: **SUPPORT**
- Allah made the Ka'bah as a place of prayer for people.
- The Ka'bah was to become a place where people bow down before Allah in worship.
- Ibrahim and Isma'il were the people Allah chose to rebuild the Ka'bah.
- Ibrahim prays that all people who believe in Allah and the Day of Judgement will be blessed.

A About three million pilgrims from all over the world attend Hajj every year. It is considered to be the largest annual gathering of people anywhere in the world

How is Hajj performed?

Hajj starts when pilgrims almost reach Makkah. They wear ihram; for men this is two sheets of white cloth wrapped around the body; women dress in simple clothes of a simple colour, usually white. The ihram is symbolic of everyone being equal before Allah.

Women must be accompanied by a man, such as a father or son, for their protection and safety. Saudi Arabian rules state that women who are under 45 and single cannot go to Hajj alone. Shi'a Muslims do not believe this condition is necessary.

> ❝**Proclaim the Pilgrimage to all people**. They will come to you on foot and on every kind of lean camel, emerging from every deep mountain pass to attain benefits and mention God's name, on specified days, over the livestock He has provided for them. **Feed yourselves and the desperately poor from them. Then let the pilgrims perform their acts of cleansing, fulfil their vows, and circle around the Ancient House**.❞ All this [is ordained by God]: anyone who honours the sacred ordinances of God will have good rewards from his Lord. ❞
>
> *(Qur'an, Surah 22: 27–30)*

1 At the start of Hajj, pilgrims perform the **tawaf** of the Ka'bah, starting from the hajar aswad (see image **C**).

This is followed by the sa'ee, a brisk walk between two hillocks called Safa and Marwah, which re-enacts Hagar's search for help when she and her son Isma'il were thirsty in the desert. When Isma'il's heels struck the ground a fountain sprouted in the shape of a well.

C Hajar aswad, a meteorite Muslims believe was sent by Allah, which is fixed to one of the corners of the Ka'bah

B A map showing the route and rituals of the Hajj pilgrimage

Makkah

Mina

6 At the end of Hajj, pilgrims sacrifice animals if they can afford it. Men shave their heads, symbolic of new life and forgiveness of past sins. Women only cut a few hairs. All end ihram by assuming normal dress, and perform a farewell tawaf.

5 Back at Mina, the ramy al-jimar takes place: each pilgrim throws pebbles at walls representing Satan (see image **D**).

Muzdalifah

4 At Muzdalifah, pilgrims collect pebbles for the ramy al-jimar in Mina the next day.

2 The pilgrims then move to Mina, four miles east of Makkah. Next morning, after the Fajr prayer, they walk nine miles to Arafat.

Arafat

3 At Arafat, the pilgrims stay in tents and spend time in reflection and prayer.

D Ramy al-jimar in Mina: Muslims stone the walls, symbolising rejection of sin and evil

'The ceremony of ramy al-jimar will not make a person less sinful.' Do you agree? Write down your response.

STRETCH

Why is Hajj important to Muslims?

- Hajj is one of the Five Pillars of Islam and must be completed by all Muslims who meet the criteria.
- It is a demonstration of unity, equality, and fraternity within Islam.
- The pilgrimage is an opportunity for all one's sins to be forgiven, so Hajj offers pilgrims a fresh start in life.

What are the benefits and challenges of Hajj?

- Hajj is a chance for individual Muslims to leave the affairs of the world for a short time and to focus on their own spirituality and relationship with Allah. A pilgrim often returns inspired, refreshed, and a changed person.
- However, it is also very demanding which is why one must be physically capable of completing all the rituals.
- Another challenge for pilgrims is to ensure that the lessons they have learned during Hajj are not forgotten in their everyday lives.

Recently many pilgrims have started to post digital self-portraits (or 'selfies') on social media sites like Twitter and Instagram while on Hajj (see image **F**). For them, it is a way of capturing a special moment in their lives. Some others would argue that taking a selfie is a distraction from the spiritual element of Hajj. They would argue that it can be a challenge to remain focused on Allah in the midst of such a significant event.

E Malik al-Shabbaz (Malcolm X) went on Hajj in 1964. He described the wonderful sense of brotherhood he felt sharing the experience with people from all over the world

 F A pilgrim takes a selfie during Hajj

BUILD YOUR SKILLS

1. With a partner or in small groups produce a guide to Hajj. This could be in the form of a large poster or a booklet. You should cover the origins and significance of Hajj, how it is performed, and its importance for Muslims.

2. 'Let the pilgrims perform their acts of cleansing, fulfil their vows, and circle around the Ancient House [Ka'bah]' (Surah 22: 29).

   Explain this verse in your own words and include what importance it has for Muslims.

3. Do you think taking a selfie is a benefit or a challenge of Hajj? Explain your view, referring to both sides of the argument.

4. Why might pilgrims re-enact Hagar's desperate search for help? Explain in 50–70 words. **STRETCH**

SUMMARY

- Hajj is one of the Five Pillars of Islam.
- The pilgrimage is compulsory for those who are physically capable and can afford all the expenses.
- Though there are challenges in completing Hajj, it brings many benefits, such as the forgiveness of sins.

 EXAM-STYLE QUESTIONS

c. Explain **two** reasons why Muslims complete Hajj. In your answer you must refer to a source of wisdom and authority. (5)

d. 'The benefits of Hajj outweigh the challenges.'
   Evaluate this statement considering arguments for and against. In your response you should:
   - refer to Muslim teachings
   - reach a justified conclusion. (15)

3.7 Jihad

SPECIFICATION FOCUS

Jihad: the origins, meaning and significance of jihad in Islam; divergent understandings of jihad within Islam, including the difference between lesser and greater jihad; the conditions for declaration of lesser jihad, including reference to Surah 2: 190–194 and 22: 39; the importance of jihad in the life of Muslims

What is jihad?

Muslims recognize that life is full of many challenges and struggles. The Arabic term for a struggle is 'juhd', which is where the word **jihad** comes from.

Often we have to make difficult choices that affect us and others too. For example, you might have to struggle with yourself when tempted to eat a chocolate cake that you know is not good for your health! Therefore, approaching various struggles in life and making wise choices are a significant aspect of a Muslim's faith.

What are the origins of jihad?

Jihad is mentioned a number of times in the Qur'an. One of the verses says:

> ❛You who believe, be mindful of God [...] and strive [jihad] for His cause, so that you may prosper.❜
> *(Qur'an, Surah 5: 35)*

Jihad is also mentioned in the Hadith.

> ❛A man came to the Prophet and asked for his permission to go for [a fighting] jihad. The Prophet asked, "Are your parents alive?" He replied, "Yes." The Prophet said, "then your jihad is with them" [by looking after them].❜
> *(Hadith – Sahih Al-Bukhari)*

USEFUL TERMS

Greater jihad: striving spiritually to resist evil within oneself

Jihad: struggle or striving

Lesser jihad: striving physically to resist an evil in the world

The Prophet Muhammad said there are two types of jihad:

- **greater jihad** (jihad al-akbar)
- **lesser jihad** (jihad al-asghar).

Greater jihad

Greater jihad is striving to resist evil within oneself and to become a better person by doing good deeds. This includes suppressing anger and helping the poor. Greater jihad is also known as the 'inner jihad'. Muslim scholars have identified some categories for this, including:

- jihad bi al-nafs (striving with the soul) – aiming to improve one's character, for example through prayer and fasting
- jihad bi al-lisan (striving with the tongue) – speaking the truth or telling others about Islam
- jihad bi al-qalam (striving with the pen) – writing about, or in defence of, your beliefs.

A Caring for one's parents is a type of jihad, according to the Hadith

Which categories of greater jihad would match with these images? **SUPPORT**

CASE STUDY: MY JIHAD

An American group of Muslims started a campaign called 'My Jihad' to show what greater jihad means to different people. They produced a series of adverts which were shown on billboards and on the side of buses.

"**#MyJihad** is to build **bridges** through **friendship**"

What's yours?

E An advert from the 'My Jihad' campaign

Why do you think they wanted to run this campaign? Find out more at **www.myjihad.org**. **STRETCH**

What would you include on your own 'My Jihad' advert? Look at the types of greater jihad on page 95 to help you. **SUPPORT**

Lesser jihad

Lesser jihad is striving to resist evil in the world through physical or military means. This includes fighting an enemy in war. Many Muslims believe that, like most nation states, they have to defend their land and faith when under attack. They are also commanded to protect places of worship belonging to other religions (Surah 22: 40).

The Prophet Muhammad sometimes took action against people who persecuted Muslims, and those who wanted to put an end to Islam. This is also known as jihad bi al-saif (striving with the sword).

The Qur'an states:

> ❝Fight in God's cause against those who fight you, but do not overstep the limits: God does not love those who overstep the limits. [...] **Fight them until there is no more persecution, and worship is devoted to God.** If they cease hostilities, there can be no [further] hostility, except towards aggressors.❞
> *(Qur'an, Surah 2: 190–194)*

> ❝Those who have been attacked are permitted to take up arms because they have been wronged❞
> *(Qur'an, Surah 22: 39)*

Muslims understand these to mean that fighting in self-defence can become necessary but that they must keep within the limits set by Allah.

F Muslims believe that lesser jihad is sometimes necessary to restore peace

Conditions for lesser jihad

Lesser jihad is allowed if:

- persecution (suffering because of your beliefs) reaches an extreme level
- religious freedoms (e.g. right to worship) are being taken away
- Islam has to be defended from an attack started by the enemy
- authorized by a Muslim leader (prophet or khalifah).

Muslims are forbidden to target innocent civilians including women, children, and the elderly; nor can the leaders of other faiths, trees, and buildings be attacked. Muslims cannot start a war, nor can fighting be used to convert people to Islam.

Interpretations of lesser jihad

Some groups, like IS and Boko Haram, believe they have a duty to fight non-Muslims so that Islam can dominate the world. They also kidnap and torture people, endorse suicide bombings, and teach that anyone who dies as a martyr (a person who dies for their beliefs) will go straight to paradise.

The majority of Muslims believe this is a wrong interpretation of jihad and that nothing can ever justify terrorism. They would emphasize the importance of peace – which is one of the meanings of the word 'Islam' – and say that lesser jihad does not permit terrorism.

> ❝ **We denounce and condemn extremism, radicalism and fanaticism today** [...] Islam is a religion of [noble] character traits in both its ends and means; a religion that strives for the good of the people, their happiness in this life and the next; and a religion that can only be defended in ways that are ethical; and the ends do not justify the means in this religion. ❞
>
> *(The Amman Declaration, a statement signed by 200 leading Muslim scholars in 2005)*

Why is jihad important to Muslims?

- Both greater and lesser jihad were practised by the Prophet Muhammad.
- The Qur'an teaches about the need to resist evil in oneself and in society.
- Allah is pleased with those who aim to improve themselves to become better people.

SUMMARY

- Jihad means to strive or to struggle.
- There are two types of jihad: greater jihad and lesser jihad.
- Greater jihad is about becoming a better person (e.g. praying); lesser jihad involves taking physical action to remove evil (e.g. fighting a war).
- Most Muslims believe greater jihad is more important than lesser jihad.

BUILD YOUR SKILLS

1 Prepare 'true' or 'false' statements about greater and lesser jihad and test each other in pairs.

2 'The strongest among you is not the one who can defeat another in fighting, but the one who can control his anger.' *(Hadith – Sahih Al-Bukhari)* **STRETCH**

   a Explain what you think this teaching means.
   b Is fighting ever justified? Explain your view and refer to Muslim teachings.

EXAM-STYLE QUESTIONS

a Outline **three** Muslim beliefs about jihad. (3)

d 'The greater jihad is more important than the lesser jihad.' Evaluate this statement considering arguments for and against. In your response you should:
- refer to Muslim teachings
- refer to different Muslim points of view
- reach a justified conclusion. (15)

What times of the year are special to you? Why are they important and how might you celebrate? Celebration happens in all societies, cultures, and religions. Islam too has special times in the year when Muslims unite to express their joy, gratitude, or commitment.

All Muslims celebrate two main festivals – **Id-ul-Adha** and **Id-ul-Fitr**. Shi'a Muslims also have two additional commemorations, known as **Id-ul-Ghadeer** and **Ashura**.

Id-ul-Adha

- Id-ul-Adha is the festival of sacrifice and commemorates the story of Ibrahim and Isma'il in the Qur'an (Surah 37: 83–111).

- Ibrahim had a dream in which he was sacrificing his son Isma'il and when he shared this with his son, the latter did not hesitate and was ready to give his life. Just as Ibrahim was about to sacrifice Isma'il, God called out to him to stop and praised both of them for their spirit of dedication. Therefore, Id-ul-Adha commemorates the obedience shown by Ibrahim and Isma'il. It is a reminder for Muslims to show a similar level of devotion.

- Id-ul-Adha was started by the Prophet Muhammad and is celebrated about ten weeks after Id-ul-Fitr and at the end of Hajj (see 3.6).

- In memory of Ibrahim and Isma'il, animals like sheep and cattle are sacrificed and their meat is shared out among the poor. Many Muslims in the UK arrange for this to be done where halal methods of slaughtering animals are followed.

- New clothes are worn and families go to the mosque to offer a special prayer and listen to a sermon. All Muslims – young and old, rich and poor – embrace each other and say 'Id Mubarak' ('Have a blessed Id'). This symbolizes community.

Id-ul-Fitr

- Id-ul-Fitr was started by the Prophet Muhammad and takes place at the end of Ramadan (see 3.4). It is a joyous occasion when Muslims express their gratefulness to Allah for being able to pass through a month that brought many blessings.

- Similar to Id-ul-Adha, new clothes are worn, families go to the mosque to offer a special prayer and listen to a sermon, and everyone says 'Id Mubarak' to each other. Gifts are exchanged and food is enjoyed in homes or in restaurants.

- The head of each family is expected to give money, which goes to less fortunate members of society so that they are not forgotten on this day.

SPECIFICATION FOCUS

The nature, origins, activities, meaning and significance of the celebration/commemoration of Id-ul-Adha, with reference to Surah 37: 77–111, and Id-ul-Fitr in Sunni Islam, with reference to their place within Shi'a Islam; and Id-ul-Ghadeer, with reference to Hadith and the interpretation of Surah 5: 3, and Ashura in Shi'a Islam, with reference to their place within Sunni Islam

USEFUL TERMS

Ashura: Shi'a commemoration of Imam Hussain's martyrdom

Id-ul-Adha: festival commemorating the devotion of Ibrahim and Isma'il

Id-ul-Fitr: festival celebrated at the end of Ramadan

Id-ul-Ghadeer: Shi'a festival commemorating the Prophet Muhammad's choice of Ali as a leader of Muslims

A Muslims, young and old, embrace each other and say 'Id Mubarak'

B Id-ul-Fitr is a joyous occasion for Muslim families

Id-ul-Ghadeer

- For Shi'a Muslims, Id-ul-Ghadeer commemorates the time they believe the Prophet Muhammad officially declared to all Muslims that Ali was to be the leader after him.

- Ghadeer is the pond where the declaration took place:

> ❛For whoever I was regarded as leader, Ali will be the leader.❜
> *(Hadith)*

SUPPORT For Shi'a Muslims, these words mean that Muhammad passed on leadership to Ali. Why do only Shi'a Muslims commemorate Id-ul-Ghadeer, and not Sunni Muslims?

- Shi'a Muslims believe this is a clear order to follow the Qur'an and the family of the Prophet after his death.

- Shi'a Muslims believe the following verse of the Qur'an has a link to Ali's appointment as leader after Muhammad (see 1.1):

> ❛Today I have perfected your religion for you, completed My blessing upon you, and chosen as your religion *islam*❜
> *(Qur'an, Surah 5: 3)*

STRETCH Why might Shi'a Muslims make a link between Id-ul-Ghadeer and Surah 5: 3?

- Shi'a Muslims are encouraged to observe a fast on this day, which takes place on the 18th of the month Dhu al-Hijjah. A gathering is held at the mosque where people recite poetry about the event and a scholar gives a speech to remind everyone about the importance of this Id. It is a day of happiness and Shi'a Muslims refer to it as the 'greatest Id'.

Ashura

- Ashura takes place on the 10th of the month of Muharram and commemorates the anniversary of the martyrdom of the Prophet Muhammad's grandson, Imam Hussain, who was murdered along with his family and companions in Karbala, Iraq ('martyrdom' is when a person is killed for their beliefs).

- Hussain refused to pledge allegiance to a leader named Yazid because he was going against the teachings of Islam and he was an oppressive ruler. Yazid wanted Imam Hussain to endorse his leadership, which forced Hussain and 72 of his relatives and companions out of Madinah where they lived. Sending an army of thousands, Yazid trapped them in the desert of Karbala where they were deprived of water and food. Eventually Yazid's army murdered most of them and took the remaining women and children captive.

C A Shi'a Muslim gives blood, organized by the National Imam Hussain Blood Donation campaign

- Shi'a Muslims commemorate this day by holding gatherings at the mosque every night from the 1st of Muharram to Ashura. Mosques are usually draped in black with the attendants also wearing black to symbolize mourning.

- Every year millions of pilgrims go to Karbala as a pilgrimage to visit the shrine of Hussain (see image **D**). Some Shi'a Muslims perform acts of self-flagellation (hitting oneself with a whip) as a way of expressing their grief. However, many Shi'a scholars have banned this as they say this is not acceptable in Islam. Many young Shi'a Muslims in Britain donate blood through the NHS in memory of Hussain (see image **C**).

- The period of mourning stops 40 days after Ashura, known as `Arba`in, when many millions more visit the shrine.

What is the significance of commemorations to Sunni and Shi'a Muslims today?

D The shrine of Imam Hussain at Karbala

For Muslims, remembering inspiring people and events from the past helps to increase their faith. Celebrations and commemorations are also a way for large sections of the ummah to unite and show their commitment to Allah in different ways. For example, for Sunni and Shi'a Muslims, occasions like Id-ul-Fitr celebrate the completion of a month of fasting, while Ashura is a time for Shi'a Muslims to reflect on the importance of honouring holy figures and opposing injustice.

BUILD YOUR SKILLS

1 Copy and complete this table for the four celebrations and commemorations.

Celebration/ commemoration	Sunni/Shi'a?	Origins	Activities	Meaning/ significance

2 'Commemorations should be happy occasions.' Do you agree? Write down your answer, and refer to Islam.

SUMMARY

- All Muslims celebrate two main festivals – Id-ul-Adha and Id-ul-Fitr. Shi'a Muslims also have two additional commemorations, known as Id-ul-Ghadeer and Ashura.

- Muslim celebrations and commemorations honour people and events in the past.

- Their purpose is to make Muslims turn more to Allah in gratitude and prayer.

EXAM-STYLE QUESTIONS

c   Explain **two** reasons why commemorations are important for Muslims. In your answer you must refer to a source of wisdom and authority. (5)

d   'All Muslims should celebrate the same commemorations.' Evaluate this statement considering arguments for and against. In your response you should:
- refer to Muslim teachings
- reach a justified conclusion. (15)

Revision

BUILD YOUR SKILLS

Look at the list of 'I can' statements below and think carefully about how confident you are. Use the following code to rate each of the statements. Be honest!

Green – very confident. What is your evidence for this?

Orange – quite confident. What is your target? Be specific.

Red – not confident. What is your target? Be specific.

A self-assessment revision checklist is available on *Kerboodle*

I can...

- List the Ten Obligatory Acts, describe what each is, and explain where they come from, referring to sources of wisdom and authority
- Explain why the Ten Obligatory Acts are important for Shi'a Muslims today and how Sunni Muslims relate to the Ten Obligatory Acts
- List the Five Pillars of Islam and explain what each of them is
- Describe the Shahadah and explain the significance of the Shahadah for Sunni and Shi'a Muslims, including reference to Surah 3: 17–21
- Explain why reciting the Shahadah is important to Muslims, and its place in Muslim practice today
- Describe Salah and explain the significance of Salah for Sunni and Shi'a Muslims, including different ways in which it is understood
- Explain what Muslims learn from Surah 15: 98–99 and Surah 29: 45
- Describe how Salah is performed including ablution, times, directions, movements, and recitations
- Describe how Salah is performed in the home, the mosque, and the Jummah prayer
- Compare and contrast the Salah with Christian forms of worship.
- Explain what Sawm is
- Explain the significance of fasting during Ramadan, including reference to Surah 2: 183–185
- Explain the purpose of fasting during Ramadan
- Explain reasons why some are excused from fasting and why
- Describe the Night of Power

- Explain the significance of the Night of Power
- Explain why Laylat al-Qadr is important for Muslims today
- Explain what Zakah is
- Explain the significance of Zakah for Sunni Muslims, including reference to Surah 9: 58–60
- Explain what Khums is
- Explain the significance of Khums for Shi'a Muslims, including reference to Surah 8: 36–42
- Explain the benefits of receiving Zakah and Khums
- Explain the origins of Hajj, with reference to sources of wisdom and authority
- Describe how Hajj is performed
- Explain the importance of Hajj for Muslims, with reference to sources of wisdom and authority
- Explain the benefits and challenges of attending Hajj
- Describe what jihad is
- Explain the origins of jihad
- Explain the differences between lesser and greater jihad, and the conditions for declaration of lesser jihad, including reference to Surah 2: 190–194 and 22: 39
- Explain the importance of jihad in the life of Muslims
- Explain the Sunni and Shi'a celebrations of Id-ul-Adha and Id-ul-Fitr, and Shi'a commemorations of Id-ul-Ghadeer and Ashura
- Explain the origins and significance of these celebrations and commemorations for Sunni and Shi'a Muslims with reference to sources of wisdom and authority, including Surah 37: 77–111 and Surah 5: 3

Exam practice

On these exam practice pages you will see example answers for each of the exam question types: **a**, **b**, **c** and **d**. You can find out more about these on pages 6–11.

• Question 'a'

*Question **a** is AO1 – it tests your knowledge and understanding.*

> (a) Outline **three** Muslim features of Zakah. (3)

Student response

Zakah is one of the Five Pillars of Islam. It requires Muslims to give 2.5% of their income to the poor, and is considered an act of worship.

Improved student response

Zakah is one of the Five Pillars of Islam. It requires Muslims to give 2.5% of their wealth, including savings or value items such as gold and silver, as long as it is above the nisab, to the poor. Zakah is an act of worship.

 Over to you! Give yourself three minutes on the clock and have a go at answering this question. Remember, an answer to an 'Outline' question does not need to include detailed explanations or reasons. You just need to state three Muslim beliefs about Zakah. A mark is awarded for each correct point.

 WHAT WENT WELL

This is a mid/high level answer. The student has understood important features of Zakah and has provided a mostly accurate response.

! HOW TO IMPROVE

Make sure you give factual information. Zakah is not paid on regular income, but on one's savings or value of items such as jewellery above the nisab. Have a look at the highlighted corrections in the improved student response.

• Question 'b'

*Question **b** is AO1 – it tests your knowledge and understanding.*

> (b) Explain **two** reasons why Hajj is important for Muslims. (4)

Student response

Hajj is an important pillar in Islam. It shows Muslims as being united.

Improved student response

Hajj is important to Muslims. Firstly, it promotes the bond of unity between Muslims of all colours and cultures. This is shown by the wearing of the ihram which symbolises the equality of all people, regardless of their background. This is seen at Hajj every year when people from Africa stand shoulder to shoulder with people from Europe, reminding Muslims that no person is superior to another person.

Secondly, Muslims believe that the pilgrimage removes all sins as long as they repent with a sincere heart. This is like being born again with a fresh start, and is symbolized with the shaving of the head. Only Allah can forgive sins, so by going on Hajj Muslims hope Allah will reward them for their commitment to him.

 WHAT WENT WELL

This is a low/mid level answer, but two correct reasons are given.

 ! HOW TO IMPROVE

Development is needed for both of the two reasons given – neither are 'explained', which is what the question specifically asks for. More time is needed to answer this question. Have a look at the level of detail given in the improved student response.

Over to you! Give yourself four minutes on the clock and have a go at answering this question. Remember, give two different points and develop each one. You could develop your points by providing an example to support each one. Avoid just repeating an earlier point.

• Question 'c'

*Question **c** is AO1 – it tests your knowledge and understanding.*

(c) Explain **two** Muslim teachings about Sawm. In your answer you must refer to a source of wisdom and authority. (5)

Student response

Muslims are taught that fasting is compulsory. The Arabic word for fasting is Sawm. This is what is taught in the Qur'an and the Hadith.

Improved student response

Sawm is one of the Five Pillars of Islam and has a close link to the month of Ramadan. Fasting is compulsory for Muslim adults who don't have any health problems. The aim of fasting is to become more 'mindful of God' (Qur'an, Surah 2: 183); in other words, to get closer to Allah through prayer. This is why some Muslims spend the last few days of Ramadan in seclusion in a mosque, called i'tikaf, free from any distractions.

Another teaching about Sawm is that it does not apply to young children, the sick and the elderly. The Qur'an teaches that 'God wants ease for you, not hardship' (Qur'an, Surah 2: 185), and so does not want to place pressure on anyone who is physically or mentally unfit to fast.

 WHAT WENT WELL

This is a low level answer, but the student has understood that Sawm is the Arabic for fasting, and that Muslims look to the Qur'an and the Hadith for guidance.

 HOW TO IMPROVE

The student needs to focus on what the question is asking. It is asking for two different Muslim teachings about Sawm to be explained. This means that the answer needs to refer to two specific teachings.

 Over to you! Give yourself five minutes on the clock and have a go at answering this question. Remember to refer to the Qur'an, Sunnah and/or the Hadith.

• Question 'd'

*Question **d** is both AO1 and AO2 – this tests your knowledge and understanding as well as your ability to evaluate. **d** questions in this section carry an extra three marks for spelling, punctuation and grammar.*

*(d) 'Laylat al-Qadr is the most important goal of a Muslim.'
Evaluate this statement, considering arguments for and against. In your response you should:
• refer to Muslim teachings
• reach a justified conclusion. (15)

Student response

I don't believe this is a true statement because one of the first questions Allah will ask a Muslim on the day of judgement will be about <u>salah</u>, not <u>laylat alqadr</u>, therefore this can't be the most important goal of a Muslim. It's not one of the Five Pillars or the six Beliefs – if it was, then you could argue that perhaps it might be one of the most important goals of a believer. I believe that experiencing <u>laylat alqadr</u> is a bonus to your belief, nothing more.

Improved student response

I don't believe this is a true statement because one of the first questions Allah will ask a Muslim on the day of judgement will be about <u>Salah</u>, not <u>Laylat al-Qadr</u> . Laylat al-Qadr (the Night of Power) is not one of the Five Pillars or the six Beliefs, nor does it feature in the 'Usul ad-Din of Shi'a Muslims, and so is not a central tenet of Islam. Muslims also try to experience it during one time of the year only – during the month of Ramadan, and even then it is in the last few days of it. Therefore, as something that makes up just a small part of a Muslim's life, Laylat al-Qadr is not viewed as one of the most important aims of a Muslim.

However, the importance of the Night of Power is clearly stated in the Qur'an and the Hadith. The Qur'an describes it as 'better than a thousand months' (Qur'an, Surah 97: 3). The Prophet Muhammad said 'only my ummah has been given Laylat al-Qadr' (Hadith – Al Durr Al Manthur) which points to its uniqueness and so it must be one of the main goals of a Muslim, as it is not experienced often. If anyone experiences it, they are extremely blessed, as the Prophet Muhammad himself experienced it at the start of Islam. In fact, there would be no Islam if his Laylat al-Qadr had not happened.

It isn't every day that angels descend from paradise, as the Qur'an says occurs during Laylat al-Qadr. This is why some Muslims spend the last few days of Ramadan in a special retreat, called i'tikaf, when they focus purely on worship so that they might be able to achieve Laylat al-Qadr. If they do, it is like having all their prayers answered.

In conclusion, there are good arguments on both sides, but I think that because Laylat al-Qadr is neither one of the Five Pillars nor one of the six Beliefs, it is not the most important duty of a Muslim. If it was, the Qur'an or the Hadith would have said it was.

 Over to you! Give yourself 15 minutes on the clock and have a go at answering this question. To begin with, read the statement in the question carefully and understand what it is saying. Show accurate understanding about Muslim beliefs and teachings, and use evidence and reasoned judgements. Aim to write five developed points and a conclusion. You cannot get more than six marks if you do not give different viewpoints.

 ✓ WHAT WENT WELL

This is a low level answer, but the student makes good points about Laylat al-Qadr not being one of the central tenets of Islam, and the importance Salah might have in comparison.

 ! HOW TO IMPROVE

The spelling, punctuation, and grammar need addressing (e.g. spelling of 'Laylat al-Qadr', and the long opening sentence). Three marks are awarded for spelling, punctuation and grammar for questions with a '*' beside them. The answer also needs an argument in favour of the statement, as well as a justified conclusion – these are provided in the improved student response opposite.

 BUILD YOUR SKILLS

In your exams, you'll need to make sure you use religious terminology correctly. Do you know the meaning of the following important terms for this topic?

Ten Obligatory Acts

Shahadah   Five Pillars

shirk   Salah

Sawm

Zakah   Laylat al-Qadr

jihad   Khums   Hajj

Chapter 4:
Matters of Life and Death

Chapter contents	Specification mapping	Page
Chapter 4: Matters of Life and Death	Section 4: Matters of Life and Death	105
4.1 Origins and value of the universe	4.1 Muslim teachings about the origins and value of the universe: scientific explanations for the origins of the universe and Muslim responses to them, including Surah 67: 1–5, including the compatibility of the Qur'an and science; divergent Muslim teachings about the value of the universe in Islam and the possible view that the universe is to be used as a commodity	107
4.2 Sanctity of life	4.2 Muslim teachings about the sanctity of life: Muslim teachings about why human life is holy; how life is shown as special in the Qur'an, including Surah 5: 32 and 4: 29; Muslim teachings on the sanctity of life; divergent understandings of the importance of sanctity of life for Muslims today	111
4.3 Origins and value of human life	4.3 Muslim response to scientific and non-religious explanations about the origins and value of human life, including evolution and survival of the fittest, including interpretations of Surah 32: 4–10 and 21: 30–33; the significance of the responses to scientific and non-religious explanations, such as evolution and survival of the fittest, for Muslims today	113
4.4 Abortion	4.4 Implications of the Muslim teachings about the value and sanctity of life for the issue of abortion: divergent Muslim teachings about the nature and use of abortion, including reference to ensoulment and Sahih Al-Bukhari 55: 549; non-religious (including atheist and Humanist) arguments surrounding its use, including the application of ethical theories, such as situation ethics, and Muslim responses to them	116
4.5 Life after death	4.5 Muslim responses to the existence of death and the afterlife: Muslim teachings and beliefs that support the existence of a life after death with reference to the Qur'an, including Surah 28: 60–80; divergent Muslim responses to arguments for life after death (including remembered lives, paranormal, logic, reward, comfort and meeting loved ones); the significance of arguments for belief in life after death for Muslims	119
4.6 Responses to arguments against life after death	4.6 Muslim responses to non-religious arguments against life after death, including Surah 45: 22–37: why Muslims reject arguments against belief in life after death (including as a source of comfort, lack of evidence, fraudulent accounts, social control)	122
4.7 Euthanasia	4.7 Implications of Muslim teachings about the value and sanctity of life for the issue of euthanasia: Muslim teachings about the nature and use of euthanasia; non-religious (inclduing atheist and Humanist) arguments surrounding its use, including the application of ethical theories, such as situation ethics, and Muslim responses to them, including Surah 2: 153–156 and including support for hospice care	126
4.8 Issues in the natural world	4.8 Muslim responses to issues in the natural world: Muslim teachings and responses to threats to the world, including pollution, global warming and the use of natural resources, including Sahih Al-Bukhari 39: 513–518; stewardship and humanity's role as khalifah; divergent Muslim responses to animal rights, including animal experimentation and the use of animals for food, including the application of ethical theories such as utilitarianism	129
Revision and Exam Practice	**Revision checklist, exam questions, sample answers and guidance**	133

4.1 Origins and value of the universe

What are the scientific explanations for the origins of the universe?

There are two opposing ideas about the origins of the universe. It has either existed for eternity, with no beginning or end, or it was created at some point in time.

The most widely held theory in science today is the Big Bang theory:

- Around 13.7 billion years ago all the matter in the universe was concentrated into a single, extremely small, intensely hot point.
- It began to expand and cool, and is still expanding today.
- Clusters of matter inside the expanding universe formed galaxies, stars, and planets, including Earth.

Evidence for the Big Bang comes from:

- background radiation, or 'ripples', in space (like shockwaves)
- galaxies moving away from us, showing that the universe is still expanding outwards from a central point.

SPECIFICATION FOCUS

Muslim teachings about the origins and value of the universe: scientific explanations for the origins of the universe and Muslim responses to them, including Surah 67: 1–5, including the compatibility of the Qur'an and science; divergent Muslim teachings about the value of the universe in Islam and the possible view that the universe is to be used as a commodity

USEFUL TERMS

Commodity: something useful or valuable

Creationist: someone who believes in the literal truth of the description of creation given in Scripture

Muslim responses

Muslims believe that Allah is the creator of everything.

> ❛Your Lord is God, who created the heavens and earth in six Days, then established Himself on the throne❜
> *(Qur'an, Surah 7: 54)*

The Arabic word yawm is usually translated as 'day'. **Creationist** Muslims believe that creation literally took place in six days, but yawm can also be a metaphor for a longer period of time.

> ❛a Day with your Lord is like a thousand years by your reckoning.❜
> *(Qur'an, Surah 22: 47)*

Many Muslims would, therefore, understand six days to mean six stages, and that the creation of everything, from the formation of galaxies to intelligent life on Earth, probably took place over billions of years.

The Qur'an also says that Allah's creation of the universe is a work of perfection:

> ❛Exalted is He who holds all control in His hands; who has power over all things; who created death and life to test you and reveal which of you does best – He is the Mighty, the Forgiving; who created the seven heavens, one above the other. **You will not see any disparity in what the Lord of Mercy creates. Look again! Can you see any cracks? Look again! And again! Your sight will turn back to you, weak and defeated.**❜
> *(Qur'an, Surah 67: 1–4)*

These verses ask people to try to find 'any cracks' or weaknesses in Allah's creation, but say that they will not be found. Their observations will be 'defeated', as the universe is a flawless creation.

Are scientific theories and the Qur'an compatible?

Some atheists might use science as a basis for arguing that Allah does not exist. For example:

- The Big Bang theory explains how the universe was created, and so it was not created by a divine being.

- There is scientific evidence for the Big Bang, but there is no scientific evidence for Allah.

- Just because human beings look for a cause or designer, it does not mean there has to be one.

Muslims believe the Qur'an was never intended to be a book of science, but that it does contain references to scientific processes which are compatible with modern ideas and theories.

There are numerous Muslim scientists who have not seen any conflict between their faith and their profession. Professor Abdus Salam, a theoretical physicist from Pakistan, made an important contribution towards the discovery of the subatomic Higgs boson particle (also called the 'God particle') present at the Big Bang. He received the Nobel Prize for Physics in 1979.

A Professor Abdus Salam often said the Qur'an inspired his scientific work

- Muslims do not believe that scientific explanations about the origins of the universe disprove Allah's existence. They would argue that all events have a cause, and that the cause of the universe was Allah.

- Many Muslims believe the Big Bang theory is compatible with their beliefs. This verse says that the heavens and the earth were 'ripped apart', and many Muslims would say that this is compatible with the idea of the 'Big Bang':

> ❜Are the disbelievers not aware that **the heavens and the earth used to be joined together and that We [Allah and the angels] ripped them apart** ❜
> *(Qur'an, Surah 21: 30)*

- Some Muslims say that scientific theories are not always right. They can also change. For instance, at one time scientists believed there was no beginning to the universe, until the Big Bang theory emerged.

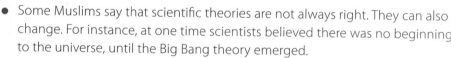

CASE STUDY: DR IMRAN MASOOD

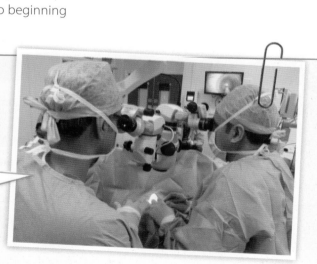

I do not believe there is a clash between science and religion. Scientists had for a long time thought that the appendix was a useless organ in the body, which made people question, why did God create it? But recently a university in the US discovered an important function for the appendix being a safe haven for good bacteria! Every day I operate on the human eye. I marvel at its intricate, yet perfect structure. This affirms in my mind the existence of God. A perfect structure could only be fashioned by a perfect creator!
(Dr Imran Masood, a Muslim consultant eye surgeon in Birmingham)

How is the universe valued in Islam?

There are many references in the Qur'an to the importance of the universe in Islam, and the many things designed by Allah to help support and sustain life.

> ❝In the creation of the heavens and earth; in the alternation of night and day; in the ships that sail the seas with goods for people; **in the water which God sends down from the sky to give life to the earth when it has been barren [...]; in the changing of the winds and clouds that run their appointed courses between the sky and earth:** there are signs in all these for those who use their minds.❞
>
> *(Qur'an, Surah 2: 164)*

Explain how the examples given in this verse are 'signs for those who use their minds.'

STRETCH

The universe as a commodity

Muslims believe that humans are the most important creation and that everything in the universe has been put in place by Allah for humans to use wisely, as a **commodity**.

> ❝There truly are signs in the creation of the heavens and the earth, and in the alternation of night and day, for those with understanding, [...] who reflect on the creation of the heavens and earth: **"Our Lord! You have not created all this without purpose"**.❞
>
> *(Qur'an, Surah 3: 190–191)*

> ❝People, worship your Lord, who created you and those before you, so that you may be mindful [of Him] who spread out the earth for you and built the sky; **who sent water down from it and with that water produced things for your sustenance.**❞
>
> *(Qur'an, Surah 2: 21–22)*

These teachings reflect the things that God has blessed humans with for their development, well-being and progress. However, many Muslims also understand these teachings to mean that this privilege should not be abused.

BUILD YOUR SKILLS

1 Outline two opposing ideas about the origins of the universe. **SUPPORT**

2 Produce a mind-map, poster, or write 300 words about the Big Bang theory. What is it, and how might it challenge belief in a divine being?

3 Why might Muslims view the universe as a commodity?

❓ EXAM-STYLE QUESTIONS

b Explain **two** Muslim beliefs about the origin of the universe. (4)

d 'I do not believe there is a clash between science and religion.'
Evaluate this statement considering arguments for and against. In your response you should:
- refer to Muslim teachings
- refer to non-religious points of view
- reach a justified conclusion. (12)

SUMMARY

- Scientists believe the universe originated 13.7 billion years ago and use the Big Bang theory to explain this.
- Some people use the Big Bang theory to argue that Allah does not exist.
- Many Muslim scientists believe Islam and science are compatible.
- The Qur'an contains many references to the origins and value of the universe.

4.2 Sanctity of life

Why is human life holy?

Muslims believe human life has been given to us by Allah. This is known as the **sanctity of life** which emphasizes that human life is holy. So, for Muslims, humans have been gifted with free will and reason, which other species have not. This gives people responsibility for their actions – how they behave towards themselves, each other, and other forms of life, including the environment and animals.

How is life shown as special in the Qur'an?

The Qur'an teaches that all life should be valued and respected. This is shown in many ways:

- **Human life should reflect the uniqueness of Allah**: Allah is described as Quddus (Holy) and Wadud (Loving). Muslims are expected to strive to show these qualities in themselves through their treatment of others.

- **You must not take a life**: 'Do not kill each other, for God is merciful to you.' (Surah 4: 29).

- **The value of one life is no less than the value of the whole human race**: 'if anyone kills a person [...] it is as if he kills all mankind, while if any saves a life it is as if he saves the lives of all mankind.' (Surah 5: 32).

- **Mankind is united in its responsibilities towards all creatures**: 'This is your community, one community – and I am your Lord: be mindful of Me' (Surah 23: 52).

- **Humans have been made trustees (khalifahs) of the earth**: Allah entrusted humans with a duty to care for his creation. 'It is He [Allah] who made you successors [khalifahs] on the earth' (Surah 6: 165). This reminds Muslims that they will be questioned in the afterlife on whether or not they fulfilled this trust.

What are other Muslim teachings on the sanctity of life?

Several Hadiths highlight the importance given to all forms of life.

- **Every person should be respected**: '"Verily your blood, your property and your honour are [...] sacred."' (Hadith – Sahih Al-Bukhari)

- **Muslims cannot harm anyone or anything**: 'The Muslim is one from whose hands and tongue the people are safe.' (Hadith – Nasa'i)

- **All human life is equally special**: In his final sermon to Muslims, the Prophet Muhammad said:

 SPECIFICATION FOCUS

Muslim teachings about the sanctity of life: Muslim teachings about why human life is holy; how life is shown as special in the Qur'an, including Surah 5: 32 and 4: 29; Muslim teachings on the sanctity of life; divergent understandings of the importance of sanctity of life for Muslims today

 USEFUL TERMS

Sanctity of life: the belief that life is holy because it is God-given

Choose one of these verses and explain in your own words what you think it means. **SUPPORT**

For each of these Hadith, explain how it links to the sanctity of life. **STRETCH**

❝**All mankind is from Adam and Eve.** An Arab has no superiority over a non-Arab, nor does a non-Arab have any superiority over an Arab; also a white person has no superiority over a black person, nor does a black person have any superiority over a white person, except by piety and good action. ❞
(Hadith)

CASE STUDY: YOUNG PLANNERS

Young Planners is an organization promoting the integration of Muslim youth in British society. As part of their 'I'm a Muslim and I give blood' campaign, they encourage Muslims to donate blood.

Islam is a religion of mercy […] It acknowledges the needs of people, thus gives concessions and dispensations wherever needed. Hence, it can be said that blood transfusion is lawful as a necessity. "And if any one saved a life, it would be as if he saved the life of all mankind." (Qur'an, Surah 5: 32)
(www.muslimsgiveblood.co.uk)

What is the importance of sanctity of life for Muslims today?

- Muslim teachings about the value of all life are important for all times, because the Qur'an's message is eternal.
- Muslims will be questioned about their treatment of others in the next life.
- Most Muslims believe that all human life is equally special, but some say that Muslim lives have a higher importance because they are part of the ummah (see 2.3).

BUILD YOUR SKILLS

1 Explain why human life is holy. Refer to teachings in the Qur'an and the Hadith in your answer.

2 Research the work of the Young Planners and show how their work is inspired by Muslim teachings. **STRETCH**

SUMMARY

- Muslims believe that all life is special.
- The Qur'an and the Hadith teach that humans have a responsibility to care for each other, and other forms of life.

❓ EXAM-STYLE QUESTIONS

a Outline **three** Muslim beliefs about why human life is holy. (3)

b Explain **two** ways life is shown as special in the Qur'an. (4)

4.3 Origins and value of human life

What are scientific and non-religious explanations about the origins and value of human life?

The most popular scientific explanation about the origin of human life is the theory of **evolution** by natural selection, attributed to nineteenth-century naturalists Charles Darwin and Alfred Russel Wallace.

- Darwin travelled extensively, observing plants and animals. He noticed small changes within species in different locations, and that completely different species inhabited different environments. For example, he observed that finches on adjacent islands showed wide variations in their size, beaks, and claws, depending on the local food source.

- Darwin's studies led him to conclude that the species we observe have not always existed in the same form, but changed gradually over a long period of time.

- Darwin noted that as the environment changed (for example, the climate got warmer or colder), the members of the species that were best suited to the new environment survived. Those that did not adapt, died out. This idea is known as **survival of the fittest**.

- The characteristics that allowed members of the species to survive passed on to the next generation.

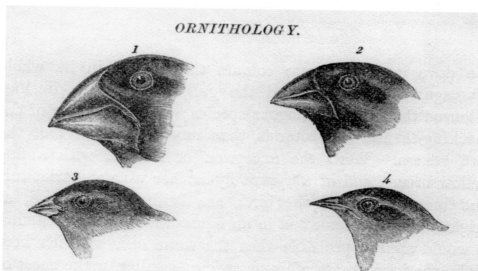

ORNITHOLOGY.

1. Geospiza magnirostris.
2. Geospiza fortis.
3. Geospiza parvula.
4. Certhidea olivacea.

Evolutionists say that humans also existed in different forms in the past. Humans share many characteristics with apes, so many conclude that humans and apes share a common ancestry. Scientists and non-religious people have a variety of views about the value of human life. Some argue that human life is worth no more than the lives of other animals and plants.

SPECIFICATION FOCUS

Muslim response to scientific and non-religious explanations about the origins and value of human life, including evolution and survival of the fittest, including interpretations of Surah 32: 4–10 and 21: 30–33; the significance of the responses to scientific and non-religious explanations, such as evolution and survival of the fittest, for Muslims today

Explain the theory of evolution in your own words.

SUPPORT

USEFUL TERMS

Evolution: the process by which different species have developed from earlier forms

Evolutionists: people who believe that life evolved from simple forms over a long period of time

Survival of the fittest: the idea that members of a species that are best suited to an environment survive

A Darwin noticed variations in the beaks of finches on adjacent islands. He concluded that finches had changed over time

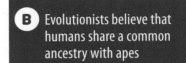

B Evolutionists believe that humans share a common ancestry with apes

'Man in his arrogance thinks himself a great work, worthy of the interposition of a deity [God]. More humble, and I believe true, to consider him created from animals.'
(Charles Darwin, 1838)

STRETCH

Explain in no more than 50 words what you think Darwin is saying. What is your view?

How do Muslims respond to these explanations?

Many parts of the Qur'an talk about how human life began, but Muslims interpret them in different ways.

> 'People, be mindful of your Lord, who created you from a single soul, and from it created its mate, and from the pair of them spread countless men and women far and wide'
> *(Qur'an, Surah 4: 1)*

This verse explains the creation of humans and their expansion across the world. In other places, the Qur'an says Allah created 'man from clay, then made his descendants from an extract of underrated fluid [semen]' (Surah 32: 7–8), and that every living thing was made from water (Surah 21: 30).

Creationist Muslims consider Adam to be the first man on earth, created by Allah 'from dust' (Surah 3: 59). Evolutionist Muslims would disagree, and believe that humans have passed through various stages of physical, intellectual, and moral development. They also say it is quite possible humans did evolve from primitive forms and that this process was part of Allah's design.

> '"What is the matter with you? Why will you not fear God's majesty, when He has created you stage by stage?"'
> *(Qur'an, Surah 71: 13–14)*

> 'You human being, what has lured you away from your generous Lord, who created you, shaped you, proportioned you, in whatever form He chose?'
> *(Qur'an, Surah 82: 6–8)*

Muslims believe that Allah has a plan for everything – there are no random occurrences without a first cause.

> 'He [Allah] placed firm mountains on the earth [...] and He spread all kinds of animals around it.'
> *(Qur'an, Surah 31: 10)*

- Many Muslims would say that this last verse is compatible with recent discoveries, such as the fossil field at Burgess Shale in the Canadian Rocky Mountains, which explains the origin of animal life during the Cambrian period, around 540 million years ago.

- Muslims believe this and other aspects of evolution prove the existence of Allah, because the Prophet Muhammad, who lived in the desert and was unable to read or write, could not have known such things centuries before scientists discovered them without this information being revealed to him by God.

All Muslims agree that human life is the most important creation, valued above all other creatures, because:

- everything else before humans (e.g. plants, seas) was prepared for human beings (see 4.1)

- Allah gave humans reason (see 4.2)

- humans have the potential to become closer to Allah

- Allah can give humans a place in heaven, unlike other species.

 C One of the many fossil finds in the Canadian Rocky Mountains. Did the Qur'an predict this amazing discovery?

What is the significance of these responses?

Many non-religious people argue that religious beliefs and teachings clash with modern scientific theories, and that this shows that holy texts are incorrect. However, evolutionist Muslims say that there are a number of verses in the Qur'an that support evidence that humans evolved, but by divine design. Muslims believe there cannot be a conflict between the *word* of God (revelation) and the *work* of God (creation).

 BUILD YOUR SKILLS

1 With a partner, take it in turns to explain different ideas about the origins of human life.

2 Explain why Muslims believe human life is to be valued above all other creatures.

3 'Evolution is how God made the world make itself.' Would a Muslim agree with this quote? What would an atheist argue? **STRETCH**

? EXAM-STYLE QUESTIONS

a Outline **three** Muslim beliefs about the origins of human life. (3)

d 'Evolution is a fact, Allah's existence is not.'
Evaluate this statement considering arguments for and against. In your response you should:
- refer to Muslim teachings
- refer to non-religious points of view
- reach a justified conclusion. (12)

 SUMMARY

- The theory of evolution by natural selection, suggests that different species, including humans, changed characteristics progressively over time due to environmental factors.

- Some people use this theory of evolution to argue that Allah does not exist.

- Creationist Muslims believe Adam was the first man, but evolutionist Muslims say that humans evolved from a simpler form by divine design.

4.4 Abortion

What is the nature and use of abortion?

Abortion – the deliberate ending of a pregnancy – is allowed under UK law as long as certain conditions are met. The 1967 Abortion Act, and amendments to this in the Human Fertilisation and Embryology Act of 1990, allow abortions in the first 24 weeks of pregnancy if:

- there is evidence that the unborn child will be severely disabled
- there is a physical or mental risk to the mother's health
- any existing children would suffer or be at risk.

Abortion is allowed after 24 weeks if the first two conditions above are met, or to prevent permanent injury to the pregnant woman. For an abortion to be carried out, two doctors must agree and it must take place in a government-approved building.

What are Muslim teachings about abortion?

Muslims believe that life is sacred and a gift from Allah, and it is not for humans to interfere in his plan for any individual.

> ❝ it is He [Allah] who gives death and life ❞
> *(Qur'an, Surah 53: 44)*

SPECIFICATION FOCUS

Implications of the Muslim teachings about the value and sanctity of life for the issue of abortion: divergent Muslim teachings about the nature and use of abortion, including reference to ensoulment and Sahih Al-Bukhari 55: 549; non-religious (including atheist and Humanist) arguments surrounding its use, including the application of ethical theories, such as situation ethics, and Muslim responses to them

USEFUL TERMS

Abortion: ending a pregnancy by deliberately removing a foetus by surgical or medical means

Conception: when the sperm and egg fertilize – the first stage of human life

Ensoulment: when the soul enters a foetus

Pro-choice: people who believe the mother should be able to choose whether to have an abortion

Pro-life: people who believe the unborn child has a right to life

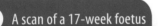

A A scan of a 17-week foetus

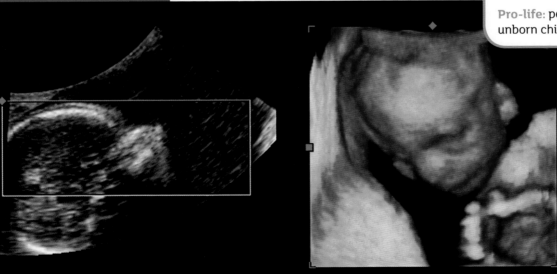

Muslims believe that life begins when one of Allah's angels blows the breath of life into the foetus. This is called **ensoulment**, and it takes place 120 days or around 17 weeks after **conception**, and is explained in the Hadith, in Sahih Al-Bukhari:

> 'Every one of you is collected in the womb of his mother for the first forty days, and then he becomes a clot for another forty days, and then a piece of flesh for another forty days. Then Allah sends an angel to write four words: He writes his deeds, time of his death, means of his livelihood, and whether he will be wretched or blessed (in religion). **Then the soul is breathed into his body.**'
>
> *(Hadith – Sahih Al-Bukhari 4: 55: 549)*

Why might this Hadith be important to Muslims? Explain in your own words. **STRETCH**

Muslims agree that if a pregnancy encounters problems and the health of the mother is at risk, her life is more important than the baby's and so an abortion is considered acceptable in such situations. However, according to the Qur'an, financial difficulties should never be an excuse for terminating a pregnancy because Muslims should trust in Allah to provide for people's needs:

> 'Do not kill your children for fear of poverty – We shall provide for them and for you – killing them is a great sin.'
>
> *(Qur'an, Surah 17: 31)*

Some Muslims quote the Qur'an's teaching that 'God does not burden any soul with more than it can bear' (Surah 2: 286) to argue that Allah would not be displeased with a couple choosing to abort if a change of circumstances following pregnancy mean that they would have difficulties raising the child.

What are non-religious arguments about abortion?

Abortion is a controversial issue for both religious and non-religious people, including atheists and Humanists. Arguments about abortion are either **pro-life** or **pro-choice**.

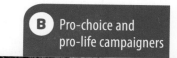

B Pro-choice and pro-life campaigners

For abortion (pro-choice)	Against abortion (pro-life)
• A foetus is not a human life until it can survive outside the womb, so abortions before around 23 weeks are not taking life.	• Every embryo has the potential for life, and should, therefore, have a right to be born.
• It is a woman's body, so she should have the right to choose what she does with it.	• Just because a baby might be disabled, does not mean it cannot live a good life.
• If a baby will not be wanted or loved when it is born, it is better for it not to be born at all.	• Giving a baby up for adoption is an alternative to an abortion. The baby could have a good life with a different family.

❝The probable quality of life of the baby, the woman, rights and wishes of the father and the rest of the family, and the doctors and nurses involved, would all have to be given due weight. There is plenty of room for debate about how much weight each individual should have, but **most humanists would probably put the interests of the woman first, since she would have to complete the pregnancy and likely care for the baby, whose happiness would largely depend on hers.**❞
(British Humanist Association)

Do you agree with this view that the mother should have the final say? Explain your answer. **SUPPORT**

Situation ethics

Those who follow situation ethics would ask: what is the most loving thing to do for all concerned? To answer this question requires careful consideration of the situation and then application of the principle of agape (love) in deciding what is in everyone's best interest. In some situations, such as an unwanted pregnancy, abortion would be the most loving act towards both the mother and the unborn baby.

Muslim responses

Abortion goes against teachings about the sanctity of life (see 4.2), and the exclusive role of Allah in giving and taking life. Many Muslims therefore regard abortion as killing. They would also consider the UK law about abortion to be a challenge to their faith. Allah is, however, merciful and he will not punish a person for ending the life of a foetus if it is to save the life of the mother.

BUILD YOUR SKILLS

1. Write down three reasons why an abortion might be allowed under UK law. **SUPPORT**

2. Which arguments are more convincing – pro-life or pro-choice? Discuss with a partner.

3. Draw a Venn diagram to show what Muslims and non-religious people might believe about abortion. Beliefs that are acceptable to both Muslims and non-religious people should appear in the area of overlap.

SUMMARY

- Abortions are legal in the UK.
- Muslims base their approach to abortion on teachings in the Qur'an and the Hadith about the sanctity of life.

? EXAM-STYLE QUESTIONS

c Explain **two** reasons why most Muslims oppose abortion. In your answer you must refer to a source of wisdom and authority. (5)

d 'If more people believed in God, there would be fewer abortions.'
Evaluate this statement considering arguments for and against. In your response you should:
- refer to Muslim teachings
- refer to relevant ethical theories
- reach a justified conclusion. (12)

4.5 Life after death

What are Muslim teachings and beliefs that support life after death?

> ❝Whatever things you have been given for the life of this world are merely [temporary] gratification and vanity: **that which is with God is better and more lasting** – will you not use your reason?
>
> Can the person who will see the fulfilment of the good promise We gave him be compared to someone We have given some enjoyments for this worldly life but who, on the Day of Resurrection, will be summoned [for punishment]? [...] **On that Day He will call them, saying, "How did you respond to My messengers?" All arguments will seem obscure to them on that Day; they will not be able to consult one another.** Yet anyone who has repented, believed, and done good deeds can hope to find himself among the successful.❞
>
> *(Qur'an, Surah 28: 60–67)*

> ❝They [disbelievers] have sworn by God with their strongest oaths that He will not raise the dead to life. But He will – it is His binding promise, though most people do not realize it❞
>
> *(Qur'an, Surah 16: 38)*

These teachings clearly state that another life is to come. This belief is often compared to our observation of the first stages of life:

> ❝Imagine the gigantic transformation from that insignificant fertilized egg into the live and kicking wonder of a baby, delivered at the end of nine months. A viewer who has not witnessed this transformation repeatedly could not at all imagine it to have happened just by looking at the first few stages of fused embryonic cells. **Life after death is likened to this amazing process – a transformation from almost nothing to a highly developed and organized form of life.**❞
>
> *(Mirza Tahir Ahmad, in Revelation, Rationality, Knowledge and Truth)*

Muslims believe in resurrection, that one day the whole of humanity will be brought back to life for the Day of Judgement (see 1.2 and 1.8).

SPECIFICATION FOCUS

Muslim responses to the existence of death and the afterlife: Muslim teachings and beliefs that support the existence of a life after death with reference to the Qur'an, including Surah 28: 60–80; divergent Muslim responses to arguments for life after death (including remembered lives, paranormal, logic, reward, comfort and meeting loved ones); the significance of arguments for belief in life after death for Muslims

USEFUL TERMS

Paranormal: unexplained things thought to have spiritual causes

Reincarnation: the belief that, after death, souls enter a new body or form

How is life after death being compared to the birth of a child? **STRETCH**

What are other arguments for life after death?

Many religious and non-religious people argue that we continue to live in some form following our death.

Remembered lives

Some believe that certain encounters and experiences enable them to recall events from a previous life. For example, someone meeting another person for the first time but feeling they may have known them before could possibly be remembering a former life. This idea of déjà vu is believed to support reincarnation, when souls are reborn into another body or form.

Paranormal

Belief in the paranormal includes a range of phenomena, from ghosts and visions of dead relatives to telekinesis (moving objects without touching them). These appear to provide evidence of the spirits or souls of the dead surviving death. Mediums and clairvoyants claim there is life after death and that they can communicate with those inhabiting the spirit world (see 4.6).

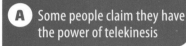
A Some people claim they have the power of telekinesis

CASE STUDY: PARANORMAL ACTIVITY

I believe that paranormal activity exists – not only as the evil portrayed in films, but as guardians. The night before [my father] passed, he came to me in a dream. He told me that he wanted to be at rest, but he needed to talk to my mother. When we arrived at the hospital later that day, I told one of my sisters about my dream. She was astounded, as she had experienced a similar vision.

That night I dreamt I was so cold and my father sat at the end of my bed. We were both crying and he just kept saying 'thank you'. I was awoken by a phone call, informing me that he had passed away. *(Irita, primary school learning mentor)*

Read about Irita and her father. Is her story convincing? Discuss with a partner. **SUPPORT**

Logic

Some people say life on earth does not make sense unless something else follows it. The idea of an afterlife appears logical to them. They may use near-death or out-of-body experiences – when a person is clinically dead for a short time and comes back to life – as evidence. They describe leaving their body and seeing themselves from above, meeting dead relatives, or seeing a bright light.

Reward

Some people believe that by living a good life, they will be rewarded with a better life elsewhere. This is not necessarily because of a god who weighs up good and bad deeds, but because of a system of justice that exists in another realm that recognizes people's actions on earth, and where something that might have been unfair is put right.

Comfort

Many people accept that there may not be enough evidence for life after death, but feel that the idea of a better existence elsewhere provides comfort at times of suffering and bereavement (see 4.6). It is also a way of looking forward to something better than this life.

Meeting loved ones

Some look forward to a time when they will be reunited with people who have been close or special to them. Often people feel that deceased loved ones are still with them and that this is evidence that they will rejoin them after death.

Muslim responses

- Muslims do not believe in reincarnation as there is no evidence for this.
- Paranormal beliefs go against the teachings of Islam.
- The idea of an afterlife reassures Muslims that they have not lived on earth without a purpose.
- Many Muslims are motivated by the promise of rewards in the akhirah for the good they have done in this life. Other Muslims do not consider this to be the only reason for performing good deeds, and consider selfless service to others for the sake of Allah as one of the highest stages of spirituality.

Why are arguments for belief in life after death significant for Muslims?

Belief in the afterlife is one of the six Beliefs of Sunni Muslims and one of the five roots of 'Usul al-Din of Shi'a Muslims (see 1.1 and 1.2). All followers of Islam believe that life has a purpose, and that how we spend our time on earth will determine what happens to us in the akhirah (see 1.8). This reminds Muslims that in the next life, they will be accountable for their actions in this world – if they have lived well, there is a better existence to look forward to.

BUILD YOUR SKILLS

1. Give two beliefs about life after death that Muslims, do not accept, and explain why.

2. 'The easiest way to come to terms with death is to invent a higher purpose.' Do you agree? Discuss your views with a partner.

SUMMARY

- There are many Muslim teachings about the existence of the afterlife.
- Many non-religious people believe that there is another life that we connect with or move on to after death.
- Muslims reject reincarnation and belief in the paranormal.

EXAM-STYLE QUESTIONS

a. Explain **two** ways that Muslims might argue for life after death. (4)

d. 'Death is a comma, not a full stop.'
Evaluate this statement considering arguments for and against. In your response you should:
  - refer to Muslim teachings
  - refer to non-religious points of view
  - reach a justified conclusion. (12)

4.6 Responses to arguments against life after death

What are the arguments against life after death and why do Muslims reject them?

Many non-religious people do not believe in life after death and say that those who do are deluding themselves or being misled. Muslims reject many of their arguments and offer reasons to believe in the afterlife.

> ❛They say, "**There is only our life in this world**: we die, we live, nothing but time destroys us." They have no knowledge of this; they only follow guesswork. Their only argument, when Our clear revelations are recited to them, is to say, "Bring back our forefathers if what you say is true."❜
> *(Qur'an, Surah 45: 24–25)*

Many non-religious people argue against life after death because of the lack of proof that anyone has come back from the dead. The Qur'an explains that the disbelievers do not understand the reality of an afterlife.

> ❛"It is God who gives you life, then causes you to die, and then He gathers you all to the Day of Resurrection of which there is no doubt, though most people do not comprehend."❜
> *(Qur'an, Surah 45: 26)*

They have also been warned about the dangers of not believing in God and the akhirah:

> ❛**When the Hour comes, those who follow falsehood will be the losers on that Day.** […] Those who believed and did good deeds will be admitted by their Lord into His mercy – that is the clearest triumph – but those who disbelieved [will be asked]: "When My revelations were recited to you, were you not arrogant and persistent in wicked deeds? When it was said to you, 'God's promise is true: there is no doubt about the Hour,' did you not reply, 'We know nothing of the Hour. This is only conjecture in our opinion. We are not convinced'?"
> **The evil of their actions will [then] become clear to them. The punishment they mocked will engulf them.**❜
> *(Qur'an, Surah 45: 27–33)*

USEFUL TERMS

Fraud: an action, or a person, that deceives someone to gain money or personal advantage

Comfort

Many people reject 'comfort' (see 4.5) as an explanation for life after death, believing the idea to be akin to fantasy:

> ❝Wouldn't it be lovely to believe in an imaginary friend who listens to your thoughts, listens to your prayers, comforts you, consoles you, gives you life after death, can give you advice? Of course it's satisfying, if you can believe it. But who wants to believe a lie?❞
> (*Professor Richard Dawkins, 'The Problem with God' interview*)

What do you think about comfort as an explanation **SUPPORT** for life after death?

Muslim responses

For Muslims, Allah is not an 'imaginary friend' but a real being with whom they can have a close relationship. Many have a deep conviction that Allah exists, and it is this that provides them with a strong faith:

> ❝truly it is in the remembrance of God that hearts find peace❞
> (*Qur'an, Surah 13: 28*)

A Professor Dawkins has long been a critic of religion and ideas about the afterlife

Lack of evidence

Many people argue that life after death cannot be scientifically proven, and so any belief in another life is based on faith, not evidence. Claims to near-death experiences (see 4.5) are dismissed as hallucinations.

CASE STUDY: AN ATHEIST PERSPECTIVE

> I'm an atheist and I don't think there is more to a person than the temporary mind and body that travels through life. No soul, no spirit. I also think that we've had a long time to produce evidence of life-after death, and everything we've put forward has been, to be polite, a little sketchy!
> (*Dr David Webster, Principal Lecturer in Religion, Philosophy and Ethics, University of Gloucestershire*)

Muslim responses

Muslims argue that their personal experience of Allah (through prayers) and the design of the universe (see 4.1) are proof of his existence, and so teachings about the afterlife must also be true. Similarly, as the Qur'an has been proven right about many things, such as scientific discoveries in modern times (see 4.3), it must also be right about the akhirah.

Fraudulent claims

Some mediums and other people who attempt to prove there is an afterlife (see 4.5) have been **frauds**, playing on the vulnerability of those who are grieving. For example, Peter Popoff, an American televangelist, claimed he was receiving revelations from God and the dead about members of his audience. In reality, his wife used a wireless radio to transmit information obtained from prayer request cards filled out by audience members before each show.

B 'Medium' Paul Popoff received 'revelations' via an in-ear receiver

Muslim responses

Many Muslims would also consider mediums to be unreliable. Islam teaches about the importance of honesty. Therefore, if someone who is truthful and trustworthy has said that they have received a message or inspiration from God, their claim should be treated seriously.

Social control

Religions are perceived by some as using the idea of paradise and hell to control people's behaviour. Historically, religious figures such as prophets have influenced people's thinking to the point that they are convinced there must be an afterlife, particularly when they have suffered for their faith. The idea of there being a hell can fill people with fear and make them behave in particular ways, purely to avoid any punishment in the afterlife.

Muslim responses

Muslims would reject this argument as humans have been given free will and cannot be forced in matters of belief:

> ❛ "Now the truth has come from your Lord: let him who wish to believe in it do so, and let those who wish to reject it do so." ❜
> (Qur'an, Surah 18: 29)

Which argument do you find most convincing, and why? Explain your reasons

STRETCH

BUILD YOUR SKILLS

1 Produce a revision mind-map or poster to show at least three arguments for and three arguments against life after death. In a different colour, add notes giving your own views on each argument.

2 'Life after death has been created in response to a human need to make sense of suffering.' Do you agree? Discuss your views with a partner.

3 What do you think the case study below is trying to show?

STRETCH

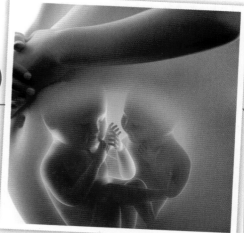

CASE STUDY: TWO BABIES IN A WOMB

In a mother's womb were two babies. One asked the other: 'Do you believe in life after delivery?' The other replied, 'Why, of course. There has to be something [...] after delivery. Maybe we are here to prepare ourselves for what we will be later.'

'Nonsense' said the first. 'There is no life after delivery. What kind of life would that be?'

The second said, 'I don't know, but there will be more light than here. Maybe we will walk with our legs and eat from our mouths. Maybe we will have other senses that we can't understand now.'

The first replied, 'That is absurd. Walking is impossible. And eating with our mouths? Ridiculous! The umbilical cord supplies nutrition and everything we need. But the umbilical cord is so short. Life after delivery is to be logically excluded.'

The second insisted, 'Well I think there is something and maybe it's different than it is here. Maybe we won't need this physical cord anymore.'

The first replied, 'Nonsense. And moreover if there is life, then why has no one ever come back from there? Delivery is the end of life, and in the after-delivery there is nothing

but darkness and silence and oblivion. It takes us nowhere.'

'Well, I don't know,' said the second, 'but certainly we will meet Mother and she will take care of us.' The first replied 'Mother? You actually believe in Mother? That's laughable. If Mother exists then where is She now?'

The second said, 'She is all around us. We are surrounded by her. We are of Her. It is in Her that we live. Without Her this world would not and could not exist.' Said the first: 'Well I don't see Her, so it is only logical that She doesn't exist.'

To which the second replied, 'Sometimes, when you're in silence and you focus and you really listen, you can perceive Her presence, and you can hear Her loving voice, calling down from above.'

SUMMARY

- Many people are not convinced there is life after death and say there is not enough evidence for it.

- There are various other reasons given for not believing in an afterlife, such as fraudulent claims by mediums, and religion being seen as a tool for social control.

- Muslims reject many of these arguments on the basis of the Qur'an and their personal experiences.

EXAM-STYLE QUESTIONS

a Outline **three** non-religious arguments against life after death. (3)

d 'People only believe in another life because it brings them comfort.'
Evaluate this statement considering arguments for and against. In your response you should:
- refer to Muslim teachings
- refer to non-religious points of view
- reach a justified conclusion. (12)

4.7 Euthanasia

What is the nature and use of euthanasia?

Euthanasia is the deliberate administering of life-ending medication by a third party.

There are two types of euthanasia:

1. Voluntary euthanasia – a person's life is ended painlessly at their own request.

2. Non-voluntary euthanasia – a person's life is ended painlessly when they are unable to ask, but there are reasonable grounds for doing so (for example, a person cannot communicate but is in extreme pain).

Euthanasia can be active. This is a deliberate action performed by a third party to kill the person (for example, by lethal injection). Active euthanasia is illegal in the UK. Doctors can also decide to withhold or withdraw medical treatment or life support that is keeping the person alive because they are not going to get better, or the person asks them to. Medical professionals call this a Non Treatment Decision. Controversially it is also sometimes called passive euthanasia. Euthanasia should not be confused with assisted dying or assisted suicide. These involve the person themselves, and not a third party, completing the final action to end their own life. Assisted dying is when the person is terminally ill and dying, and assisted suicide is when the person is seriously ill but not dying.

What are Muslim teachings about euthanasia?

The large majority of Muslims are against euthanasia. They believe that life is a test. So, while many people may face very difficult situations, they are expected to remain strong in their faith, and not kill themselves or have others assist them to die.

SPECIFICATION FOCUS

Implications of Muslim teachings about the value and sanctity of life for the issue of euthanasia: Muslim teachings about the nature and use of euthanasia; non-religious (including atheist and Humanist) arguments surrounding its use, including the application of ethical theories, such as situation ethics, and Muslim responses to them, including Surah 2: 153–156 and including support for hospice care

USEFUL TERMS

Euthanasia: the deliberate administering of life-ending medication by a third party

Hospice care: a style of care that aims to improve the lives of people who have an incurable illness

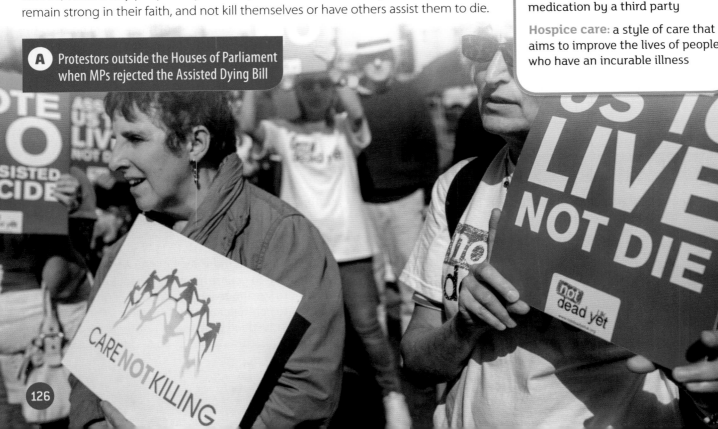

A Protestors outside the Houses of Parliament when MPs rejected the Assisted Dying Bill

Many Muslims believe that if a person's survival depends on a life-support machine, and nothing further can be done for them, then the machine should be turned off to allow nature to take its course.

'If it is scientifically certain that life cannot be restored, then it is futile to diligently keep the patient in a vegetative state by heroic means or to preserve the patient by deep freezing or other artificial methods.'
(The Islamic Code of Medical Ethics, 1981)

STRETCH Read this quotation. What is it arguing? Can you think of any arguments against this perspective?

What are non-religous arguments about euthanasia?

Euthanasia is a controversial issue for non-religious people, including atheists and Humanists. Those who support euthanasia believe:

- the patient can die with dignity rather than continuing to live with a poor quality of life

- euthanasia allows the patient to die as they choose

- helping a person die can save medical costs, which can instead be spent on others

- the relatives can be relieved from the emotional and financial burden of taking care of a terminally ill person.

Situation ethics focuses on the law of love as the best way of deciding what to do in particular circumstances. A question that a situation ethicist would therefore ask about euthanasia is: 'Is it the most loving thing for everyone involved?'

SUPPORT Which of these arguments do you think is the most convincing, and why? Discuss with a partner and give reasons for your answer.

Muslim responses

Most Muslims would disagree with these arguments because:

- they believe in the sanctity of life (see 4.2)

- ending human life by our own will is 'playing God'

- some patients may feel pressured into dying in order not to be a burden on their families and carers.

'You who believe, seek help through steadfastness and prayer, for God is with the steadfast [...] **We shall certainly test you with fear and hunger [...] But [Prophet], give good news to those who are steadfast**, those who say, when afflicted with a calamity, "We belong to God and to Him shall we return."'
(Qur'an, Surah 2: 153–156)

B Islam teaches Muslims to respect and take care of their parents

SUPPORT Copy out these verses and explain what they are teaching in your own words. Discuss your ideas with a partner and agree on a final meaning.

Muslims also believe that taking care of their parents and relatives in old age is a special duty, and an opportunity to serve them for however long Allah keeps them on earth.

❝Your Lord has commanded that [...] you **be kind to your parents.** If either or both of them reach old age with you, say no word that shows impatience with them, and do not be harsh with them, but **speak to them respectfully and lower your wing in humility towards them in kindness** and say, "Lord, have mercy on them, just as they cared for me when I was little." ❞

(Qur'an, Surah 17: 23–24)

'**Lower your wing in humility**' means to show compassion. **SUPPORT**

The Prophet Muhammad strongly condemned those who had the opportunity to serve their parents in old age, but failed to do so.

Due to the importance given to taking good care of one's parents, many Muslims support **hospice care**. This provides for a person's medical, emotional, social, practical, psychological and spiritual needs, during their remaining time on earth. The aim is that, as a result, they will be less likely to contemplate euthanasia. Hospice care can be provided at the person's own home or in a care home.

BUILD YOUR SKILLS

1   What is euthanasia?

2   How do non-religious people that support euthanasia view it? Do you agree with their views? Give reasons for your opinion, showing you have considered how non-religious people would respond to the issue of euthanasia.

SUPPORT

3   Research the case of either Tony Nicklinson or Lynn Gilderdale. Produce a report of what happened and include how Muslims would feel about it.

STRETCH

SUMMARY

- Euthanasia is illegal in the UK.
- Muslims base their approach to euthanasia on teachings in the Qur'an and the Hadith about the sanctity of life.
- Many Muslims support hospice care for the terminally ill.
- Non-religious people that support euthanasia argue that the patient has a right to die as they choose.

C An increasing number of British Muslims are expected to use hospice care as working relatives find it harder to provide the care they need at home

EXAM-STYLE QUESTIONS

a   State **three** features of hospice care. (3)

c   Explain **two** reasons why most Muslims oppose euthanasia. In your answer you must refer to a source of wisdom and authority. (5)

4.8 Issues in the natural world

To Muslims, the sanctity of life is important (see 4.2). Allah is the creator of everything, including the earth, and humans have a responsibility to ensure that they take good care of the planet. However, this does not always happen.

What threats are there to the natural world?

There are many factors endangering the environment:

- **Pollution**: this refers to anything that contaminates the soil, water, landscape, or atmosphere. It is usually caused by waste, particularly waste created by our industrialized lifestyle, and it is having a detrimental effect on our planet.
- **Global warming**: this is the increase in temperature on Earth resulting from human activity. It is also called the greenhouse effect because the gases created from burning coal, oil and gas create a 'blanket' around the Earth, making the Earth warmer. Global warming is causing ice caps to melt, sea levels to rise, and extreme weather to become more common.
- **Use of natural resources**: these are plants, animals and minerals that occur naturally on Earth, which humans are using at an alarming rate. For example, commercial fishing is upsetting the natural balance of the marine ecosystem (an ecosystem is the relationship between the living and non-living components in an environment).

What are Muslim teachings and responses to these threats?

Islam teaches that humanity has been made a khalifah, or trustee, of the Earth. The world is a gift from Allah and it is our responsibility to maintain the harmony and balance that he created. We must also look after it for the next generation. This is known as **stewardship**. Muslims believe that they will be accountable for this in the akhirah (see 1.8), which affects the way they live now.

> ❝It is he [Allah] who made you successors [khalifahs] on the earth❞
> *(Qur'an, Surah 6: 165)*

SPECIFICATION FOCUS

Muslim responses to issues in the natural world: Muslim teachings and responses to threats to the world, including pollution, global warming and the use of natural resources, including Sahih Al-Bukhari 39: 513–518; stewardship and humanity's role as khalifah; divergent Muslim responses to animal rights, including animal experimentation and the use of animals for food, including the application of ethical theories such as utilitarianism

USEFUL TERMS

Stewardship: taking care of the Earth as khalifahs (trustees) on behalf of God and for the next generation

Utilitarianism: the idea that whatever promotes the greatest good or happiness for the greatest number of individuals is what is morally right

A Water becomes polluted with litter and toxic substances

Muslim teachings guide believers to make sure that the Earth is protected and respected, and that natural resources are used sensibly, not wasted. For this reason, many Muslims support conservation projects and recycling.

> ❝There is none amongst the Muslims who plants a tree or sows seeds, and then a bird, or a person or an animal eats from it, but is regarded as a charitable gift for him.❞
> *(Hadith – Sahih Al-Bukhari 39: 513)*

How does this Hadith relate to a Muslim's role as a khalifah? Explain your answer. Research Sahih Al-Bukhari 5: 514–518 to extend your answer.

STRETCH

CASE STUDY: MUSLIMS FOR HUMANITY

Muslims for Humanity is a scheme run by young British Ahmadiyya Muslims who have been inspired by the Hadith in Sahih Al-Bukhari to help provide volunteers to plant more than 140,000 trees around the UK. Volunteer Mahmood Razzaq said: 'We are committed to doing our bit to improve the environment and beautify the local communities we live in. It is a cause close to our hearts because Islam places enormous emphasis on taking care of the environment'.
(www.muslimsforhumanity.org.uk)

What are divergent Muslim responses to animal rights?

Islam recognizes the value of animals as part of the created world. They have been given a special purpose by Allah and so should be treated with respect. Muslims, therefore, have strong views about animal experimentation and the use of animals for food.

B Protestors campaigning against the misuse of animals

Animal experimentation

There are no direct teachings about animal experimentation in the Qur'an or the Hadith, so Muslims use the principles of kindness and compassion, and also stewardship, to help them decide where they stand on this issue.

Many Muslims believe that animal experimentation is acceptable if it is for a good purpose, such as helping to increase human understanding and the development of medicine, which can help provide cures for illnesses. Animals must still be treated humanely. Muslims oppose experimenting on animals for luxuries, such as cosmetics, or anything that creates unnecessary suffering.

> ❛Whoever kills a sparrow or anything bigger than that without a just cause, God will hold him accountable on the Day of Judgement.❜
> *(Hadith – Nasa'i)*

Use of animals for food

> ❛It is He [Allah] who made the sea of benefit to you: you eat fresh fish from it❜
> *(Qur'an, Surah 16: 14)*

> ❛[He gave you] livestock, as beasts of burden and as food. So eat what God has provided for you and do not follow in Satan's footsteps❜
> *(Qur'an, Surah 6: 142)*

These verses show that some animals have been created for humans to eat. Food and drink in Islam are divided into three main categories:

- **Halal**: permitted and prepared according to Muslim teachings.
- **Tayyab**: pure and wholesome.
- **Haram**: forbidden, such as pork.

For meat to be halal, it needs to be farmed and slaughtered according to Islamic guidelines. This involves cutting the animal's throat quickly but humanely, to reduce the pain inflicted. The name of Allah must be recited and all blood drained from the carcass. Animals should not be shown the knife, or be slaughtered in front of other animals, so as not to unsettle them.

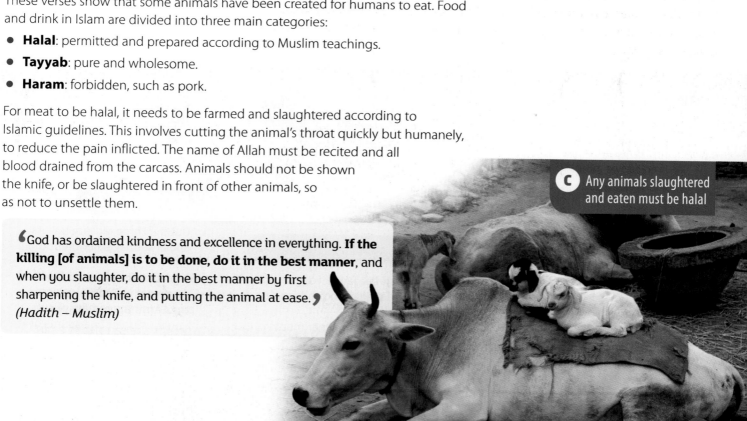

C Any animals slaughtered and eaten must be halal

> ❛God has ordained kindness and excellence in everything. **If the killing [of animals] is to be done, do it in the best manner**, and when you slaughter, do it in the best manner by first sharpening the knife, and putting the animal at ease.❜
> *(Hadith – Muslim)*

Muslims believe that there is a close link between the physical, moral, and spiritual. While certain foods are halal, others are haram, as it is believed they are impure. Meat that Muslims must not consume includes:

- carrion, blood, pork, and anything sacrificed in the name of any god other than Allah (Surah 2: 173)
- that which is strangled, gored to death, the victim of a violent blow or fall, or sacrificed upon an altar to idols (Surah 5: 3).

While the majority of Muslims eat halal meat, some Muslims choose to be vegetarians.

Why might Muslims have these rules about what they can and cannot consume? **STRETCH**

Utilitarianism and animal rights

There are various ethical theories that try to guide people on how to reach moral decisions. One of these is **utilitarianism**. Utilitarianism promotes the greatest good or happiness for the greatest number of individuals, which means that whatever satisfies, or is in the best interests of, most people is what is morally right. Some utilitarians have used this principle to justify the use of animal experimentation and the use of animals for food, because they are useful to human beings; others disagree. A famous utilitarian philosopher, Peter Singer, campaigns for the moral rights of animals and for animals to be recognized as 'persons' just like humans. He came up with the expression 'speciesism', which applies when humans do not treat other species with equal respect.

> ❝ To give preference to the life of a being simply because that being is a member of our species would put us in the same position as racists who give preference to those who are members of their race. ❞
> (Peter Singer, Practical Ethics)

BUILD YOUR SKILLS

1. Outline three threats to the natural world.

SUPPORT

2. How are Muslims responding to these threats? Refer to Muslim teachings in your answer.

3. Is animal experimentation always right? Discuss with a partner.

4. Do you agree with Peter Singer? Share your thoughts in a group.

SUMMARY

- Muslims believe they are God's khalifahs (trustees) on earth.
- Muslims are taught to show care and compassion towards animals.
- There are different Muslim views about the use of animals for experiments and food.

? EXAM-STYLE QUESTIONS

a Outline **three** Muslim beliefs about animal experimentation. (3)

c Explain **two** ways that Muslims might act as khalifahs of the Earth. In your answer you must refer to a source of wisdom and authority. (5)

Revision

BUILD YOUR SKILLS

Look at the list of 'I can' statements below and think carefully about how confident you are. Use the following code to rate each of the statements. Be honest!

Green – very confident. What is your evidence for this?

Orange – quite confident. What is your target? Be specific.

Red – not confident. What is your target? Be specific.

A self-assessment revision checklist is available on *Kerboodle*

I can...

- Give scientific explanations for the origins of the universe and explain Muslim responses, including reference to Surah 67: 1–5 and the compatibility of the Qur'an and science

- Give divergent Muslim teachings about the value of the universe in Islam and how the universe can be used as a commodity

- Explain Muslim teachings about why human life is holy, and how life is shown as special in the Qur'an, including reference to Surah 5: 32 and 4: 29

- Explain Muslim teachings on the sanctity of life, including divergent understandings of the importance of sanctity of life for Muslims today

- Give Muslim responses to scientific and non-religious explanations about the origins and value of human life, including evolution and survival of the fittest, including interpretations of Surah 32: 4–10 and 21: 30–33

- Explain the significance of Muslim responses to scientific and non-religious explanations about the origins and value of human life for Muslims today

- Give divergent Muslim teachings about the nature and use of abortion, including reference to ensoulment and Sahih Al-Bukhari 55: 549

- Give non-religious (including atheist and Humanist) arguments surrounding the use of abortion and explain how ethical theories, such as situation ethics, can be applied to the issue

- Explain Muslim responses to non-religious attitudes to the use of abortion and the application of ethical theories, such as situation ethics, to the issue

- Explain Muslim teachings and beliefs that support the existence of life after death with reference to the Qur'an, including Surah 28: 60–80

- Give arguments for life after death, including remembered lives, paranormal beliefs, logic, reward, comfort and meeting loved ones

- Give divergent Muslim responses to arguments for life after death and explain the significance of arguments for belief in life after death for Muslims

- Explain why Muslims reject non-religious arguments against belief in life after death – including as a source of comfort, lack of evidence, fraudulent accounts and social control – with reference to Surah 45: 22–37 and other teachings

- Explain Muslim teachings about the nature and use of euthanasia

- Give non-religious (including atheist and Humanist) arguments surrounding the use of euthanasia

- Explain how ethical theories, such as situation ethics, can be applied to the issue of euthanasia

- Explain Muslim responses to non-religious attitudes to the use of euthanasia and the application of ethical theories, such as situation ethics, to the issue, with reference to Surah 2: 153–156 and support for hospice care

- Explain Muslim teachings and responses to threats to the world, including pollution, global warming and the use of natural resources, including reference to Sahih Al-Bukhari 3: 513–518

- Explain Muslim teachings about stewardship and humanity's role as khalifah

- Give divergent Muslim responses to animal rights, including animal experimentation and the use of animals for food

- Apply ethical theories such as utilitarianism to the issue of animal rights

Exam practice

On these exam practice pages you will see example answers for each of the exam question types: **a**, **b**, **c** and **d**. You can find out more about these on pages 6–11.

• Question 'a'

*Question **a** is AO1 – it tests your knowledge and understanding.*

> (a)   State **three** arguments for belief in life after death. (3)

Student response

- *Reward*
- *Paranormal*

Improved student response

Three arguments for life after death are reward, the paranormal and remembered lives.

 Over to you! Give yourself three minutes on the clock and have a go at answering this question.

 ✓ **WHAT WENT WELL**

This is a mid level answer. The student has given two correct responses.

 ❗ **HOW TO IMPROVE**

A third correct response is needed. The answer could also be improved by writing it as a sentence rather than bullet points – as seen in the improved student response.

• Question 'b'

*Question **b** is AO1 – it tests your knowledge and understanding.*

> (b)   Explain **two** Muslim teachings about stewardship. (4)

Student response

Muslims believe that humans are khalifahs, or trustees, of the earth. This means that they should take care of the planet on behalf of Allah, who has entrusted them with this responsibility.

Improved student response

Muslims believe that humans are khalifahs, or trustees, of the earth. This means that they should take care of the planet on behalf of Allah, who has entrusted them with this responsibility. It is a role that must be taken seriously.

Additionally, Muslims are required to leave the earth in a good state for future generations who will inherit the earth. They will be accountable in the akhirah for how they fulfilled this role. One way Muslims explain the importance of this responsibility is by asking, 'Wouldn't you want to pass on to your own children, grandchildren etc. something that they will be thankful for?'

 Over to you! Give yourself four minutes on the clock and have a go at answering this question.

 ✓ **WHAT WENT WELL**

This is a mid level answer. It contains a good explanation about the idea that Allah entrusted humans to take care of the earth.

 ❗ **HOW TO IMPROVE**

This student needs to include a second explanation, which is missing from this answer. Remember to read the question carefully and provide exactly what you are being asked for – see the improved student response opposite.

• Question 'c'

*Question **c** is AO1 – it tests your knowledge and understanding.*

> (c) Explain **two** Muslim beliefs about science. In your answer you must refer to a source of wisdom and authority. (5)

Student response

There is no way that Islam and science can be compatible. I believe in evolution and although a lot of Muslims are also evolutionists, there is no way that you can believe in Allah and also in science. There is always proof for scientific theories, but not for religious beliefs. The existence of Allah is a matter of faith, not evidence.

Improved student response

There are many Muslims who believe that Islam is compatible with science. This is because the Qur'an refers to aspects of evolution that agree with modern theories about the origins of animal and human life. For example, Surah 71: 14 states that Allah created people in stages, which supports scientific ideas about humans passing through various stages of physical development.

Muslims also believe that Allah is the first cause and that there are no random occurrences in nature. As Surah 82: 6–7 teaches, 'Your generous Lord, who created you, shaped you, proportioned you'. This teaches Muslims that Allah directs every stage of our growth, and does not go against anything scientists say about the process of human development.

 Over to you! Give yourself five minutes on the clock and have a go at answering this question.

 WHAT WENT WELL

This is a low level answer. The student recognises that many Muslims believe in evolution.

 HOW TO IMPROVE

This is an 'Explain Muslim beliefs' question so should not include a personal opinion. It must also refer to a source of wisdom and authority, which can be seen in the improved student response opposite.

• Question 'd'

*Question **d** is both AO1 and AO2 – this tests your knowledge and understanding as well as your ability to evaluate.*

> (d) 'There is no evidence for life after death.'
> Evaluate this statement, considering arguments for and against. In your response you should:
> • refer to Muslim teachings
> • refer to non-religious views
> • reach a justified conclusion (12)

Student response

There are many convincing arguments to support this statement. Evidence is extremely important to prove whether what someone believes is true or not, and life after death is one of those things that nobody has been able to prove exists. Some people have claimed to have had out of body experiences but these can be scientifically explained as having been caused by chemical reactions when brains lack oxygen. Nobody has returned from the dead to tell us about the afterlife.

Many people also make fraudulent claims, like the guy in America who tricked people into thinking that he was receiving messages from God but was actually getting messages sent to his ear piece!

However, there are many people who believe in remembered lives, which is the idea that they have lived a previous existence and can recall things from that life. Other people say that because this life is unfair and lots of injustices take place, it is logical that there must be another life after death where people will be rewarded for how they have lived. Overall, I agree with the non-religious position that there is not enough evidence of an afterlife, as it comes down to faith rather than any proof.

Improved student response

There are many convincing arguments to support this statement. Evidence is extremely important to prove whether what someone believes is true or not, and life after death is one of those things that nobody has been able to prove exists. Some people have claimed to have had out of body experiences but these can be scientifically explained as having been caused by chemical reactions when brains lack oxygen. Nobody has returned from the dead to tell us about the afterlife. Many people also make fraudulent claims, like Paul Popoff in America, who tricked audiences into thinking that he was receiving revelations from God when he was actually getting messages from his wife sent to his ear piece! This was exposed in the media.

However, there are many people who believe in remembered lives, which is the idea that they have lived a previous existence and can recall things from that life. Other people say that because this life is unfair and lots of injustices take place, it is logical that there must be another life after death where people will be rewarded for how they have lived.

Muslims would say that the Qur'an is the perfect word of God and so everything that it contains must be true. It refers to the akhirah, so this should be sufficient evidence for life after death. Muslims believe that we have free will, and so must be accountable for the things that we do. All our actions will be judged in the next life where 'people will be separated' (Qur'an, Surah 30: 14) – those who have done good things are promised jannah, whilst those who commit evil will earn jahannam. Muslims believe that there is evidence for the soul and this is immortal, therefore whilst the body decays, spiritually we continue to live, and must therefore go on to the akhirah, otherwise our lives would be meaningless.

The Qur'an also addresses the criticisms of non-believers and says that they lack proper understanding: 'It is God who gives you life, then causes you to die, and then He gathers you all to the Day of Resurrection of which there is no doubt, though most people do not comprehend.' (Qur'an, Surah 45: 26).

Overall, I agree with the non-religious position that there is not enough evidence of an afterlife, as it comes down to faith rather than any proof.

Over to you! Give yourself 12 minutes on the clock and have a go at answering this question.

✓ WHAT WENT WELL

This is a mid level answer. Different viewpoints, including non-religious arguments, have been given. The answer reflects a clear understanding of the positions held by different people, and their reasons for believing in them.

! HOW TO IMPROVE

Other than being too short an answer, there is no reference to Muslim beliefs, therefore the answer will not gain many marks – see the improved student response opposite.

BUILD YOUR SKILLS

In your exams, you'll need to make sure you use religious terminology correctly. Do you know the meaning of the following important terms for this topic?

creationist

sanctity of life

evolution

ensoulment

paranormal

reincarnation

euthanasia

stewardship

Glossary

Abortion ending a pregnancy by removing a foetus by surgical or medical means

Adalat Divine justice. Also known as 'Adl

Adhan the call to prayer in Aarabic

Adultery sex where one or both of those involved are already married to someone else (extramarital sex)

Ahl al-bayt people of the Prophet Muhammad's house (family)

Akhirah life after death, when the Day of Judgement takes place

Al-Qadr (predestination) belief that Allah has preordained certain things and put in place fixed universal laws

Allah Arabic name for God

Amr bil ma'roof encouraging good action

Annulment when it is declared that a marriage was never valid

Aqiqah a ceremony marking the birth of a newborn baby

Ashura Shi'a commemoration of Imam Hussain's martyrdom

Barzakh stage between death and the time of judgement

Beneficence kindness, generosity

Blended family two families uniting when parents meet new partners

Cohabitation living together while not married

Coitus interruptus when the penis is removed from the vagina before ejaculation

Commodity something useful or valuable

Conception when the sperm and egg fertilize – the first stage of human life

Contraception the deliberate prevention of pregnancy

Creationist someone who believes in the literal truth of the description of creation given in Scripture

Divorce legally ending a marriage

Ensoulment when the soul enters a foetus

Euthanasia the deliberate administering of life-ending medication by a third party

Evolution the process by which different species have developed from earlier forms

Evolutionists people who believe that life evolved from simple forms over a long period of time

Family planning when a couple consider whether or not to have a child

Five Pillars the most important duties of a Muslim; known as Arkaan al-Islam

Fraud an action, or a person, that deceives someone to gain money or personal advantage

Gender prejudice believing that one gender is less or more important than another

Gender discrimination treating people less or more favourably because of their gender

Greater jihad striving spiritually to resist evil within oneself

Hadith sayings of the Prophet Muhammad

Hajj the pilgrimage made by Muslims to Makkah

Homosexuality sexual relations between two people of the same sex

Hospice care a style of care that aims to improve the lives of people who have an incurable illness

Humanity all human beings

I'tikaf a period of retreat in the mosque during the last ten days of Ramadan for worship

Id-ul-Adha festival commemorating the devotion of Ibrahim and Isma'il

Id-ul-Fitr festival celebrated at the end of Ramadan

Id-ul-Ghadeer Shi'a festival commemorating the Prophet Muhammad's choice of Ali as a leader of Muslims

Imam person who leads Salah

Immanence a belief that Allah acts in the world

Injil original Gospel of Isa

Jihad struggle or striving

Jummah prayer congregation held every Friday, usually in the mosque

Ka'bah cube-shaped building in Makkah which Muslims believe was the first house of Allah on earth, rebuilt by Ibrahim and Isma'il

Khalifah a religious leader (caliph), representing Allah or a prophet

Khitan male circumcision, when a baby's foreskin is removed for health reasons

Khums a system for Shi'a Muslims to pay an additional 20 per cent of their savings towards community causes

Kiraman katibin noble scribes, the angels who note every person's good and bad deeds

Kitab al-iman the Book of Faith in the Sahih Muslim collection of Hadith

Kutubullah books of Allah

Laylat al-Qadr the Night of Power

Lesser jihad striving physically to resist an evil in the world

Malaikah the Arabic name for angels

Mi'ad the Day of Judgement and the Resurrection

Miracles extraordinary events that may not be explainable

Nahi anil munkar discouraging evil actions

Nikah marriage contract

Nisab the amount of wealth above which a Muslim needs to pay Zakah

Nuclear family mother, father, and children living as one unit

Omnipotence being all-powerful

Paranormal unexplained things thought to have spiritual causes

Pilgrimage a journey to a place which is special for religious reasons

Premarital sex a sexual relationship which occurs before marriage

Pro-choice people who believe the mother should be able to choose whether to have an abortion

Pro-life people who believe an unborn child has a right to life

Procreation having children

Prophet a messenger chosen by Allah to teach humanity what is right and wrong

Qiblah the direction Muslims face (towards Makkah) during Salah

Qur'an the holiest text in Islam

Rak'ah set of movements and words in each Salah

Ramadan month of fasting, one of the pillars of Islam

Reincarnation the belief that, after death, souls enter a new body or form

Remarriage marrying again after being divorced from a previous marriage

Resurrection the belief that humans will be raised again in the next life

Revelation communication from Allah, often through an angel

Risalah the system of communication between Allah and people, through prophets

Sadaqah voluntary charity, not fixed at any rate

Sahifah scrolls of Ibrahim and Moses

Salah the Muslim prayer

Sanctity of life the belief that life is holy because it is God-given

Sawm to 'keep away' from something, also known as fasting

Scripture a holy book or text given by Allah through a prophet

Shahadah declaration of belief, which Muslims are required to say

Shari'ah Islamic legal system based on Muslim scholars' understanding of the Qur'an, Sunnah and the Hadith

Shi'a Muslims who believe that leadership belongs to the ahl al-bayt

Shirk a sin that involves setting up equals to Allah; worshipping anyone or anything besides him

Sin an action against Allah's will

Situation ethics the idea that people should base moral decisions on what is the most loving thing to do

Stewardship taking care of the Earth as khalifahs (trustees) on behalf of God and for the next generation

Sunni Muslims who believe Abu Bakr was the first of four 'rightly guided' leaders after the Prophet Muhammad

Surah chapter

Surrogacy when a woman becomes pregnant and gives birth for a couple who are unable to have children

Survival of the fittest the idea that members of a species that are best suited to an environment survive

Tawaf anti-clockwise circuit of the Ka'ba, completed seven times during Hajj

Tawhid belief in one God; in the oneness of Allah

Tawrat Torah

Ten Obligatory Acts the most important duties of a Shi'a Muslim

Transcendence a belief that Allah is above and beyond his creation

Ummah community of Muslims around the world

'Usul ad-Din name given to the principles of faith in Shi'a Islam

Utilitarianism the idea that whatever promotes the greatest good or happiness for the greatest number of individuals is what is morally right

Wudu' purification ritual to ensure one is clean before prayer

Zakah literally 'purification' (of wealth), one of the pillars of Islam

Zabur Psalms of David

Index

A

abortion **116–18**
Abraham **25, 28, 92**
Adalat (Divine Justice) **19, 23**
Adam **24–5**
adhan **55**
adultery **49, 50**
afterlife **37–40, 119–25**
ahl al-bayt **16**
akhirah (afterlife) **34, 36, 37–40, 122–3**
al-Qadr (predestination) **34–6**
Ali, Imam **16, 80**
Allah **17, 19, 21–3, 34, 80, 108, 114, 123**
Amr bil ma'roof **77, 78**
angels **31–3**
animal rights/welfare **130–2**
annulment of marriage **61**
aqiqah **56**
Ashura **98, 99–100**
atheists **60, 62, 109, 123**

B

barzakh **37**
beneficence **21–2**
Big Bang theory **107, 109**
birth control **59–60**
blended families **53**
Britain
    Islam in **13**
    marriage **48**
    religious beliefs **12**

C

caliph (khalifah) **16**
celebrations **98–100**
charity **89–91**
children **53, 56**
circumcision **55, 56**
cleansing **82, 84**
cohabitation **47, 48**

coitus interruptus **59, 60**
commemorations **98–100**
commodities **107, 110**
community activities **55–8**
conception **116, 117**
contraception **59–60**
counselling **56–7**
Creationists **107, 108, 114**

D

Darwin, Charles **113, 114**
Dawud (David) **26, 29**
Day of Judgement **20, 36, 37–9**
death **32, 56**
    see also afterlife
discrimination **67–70**
Divine Justice **19, 23**
divorce **61–3**

E

elderly people, care of **127, 128**
ensoulment **116, 117**
equality of men and women **64–70**
ethics **59, 60, 63, 118, 127, 132**
euthanasia **126–8**
Eve **25**
evolution **113–15**
evolutionists **113**
extremism **97**

F

fairness **23**
the family **52–8**
family planning **59–60**
fasting **85–8**
festivals **98–100**
Five Pillars of Islam **79, 92**
food **131–2**
fraud **122, 124**
free will **35–6**
Friday prayer (Jummah) **84**

G

Gabriel **31, 32, 33**
gender prejudice **67–70**
global warming **129**
Gospel **29**
greater jihad **95**

H

Hadith **16–18, 95, 111–12, 117**
Hajj **92–4**
halal foods **131**
haram foods **131, 132**
Hawwa (Eve) **25**
heaven **38, 124**
hell (jahannam) **38–9, 124**
holy books **28–30**
home worship **84**
homosexuality **49, 50–1**
hospice care **126, 128**
human freedom **35–6**
human life, origins of **113–15**
Humanists **60, 62, 118**
humanity **24**
Hussain, Imam **99**

I

Ibrahim (Abraham) **25, 28, 92**
Id-ul-Adha **98**
Id-ul-Fitr **98**
Id-ul-Ghadeer **98, 99**
Imamah **19–20**
Imams **16, 19, 84**
immanence **21–2**
Injil (Gospel) **29**
Isa (Jesus) **26–7, 29**
Ishmael **25–6**
Isma'il (Ishmael) **25–6**
i'tikaf **85, 88**
Izra'il **32**

J

jahannam (hell) **38–9, 124**
jannah (paradise) **38, 124**
Jesus **26–7, 29**
Jibril (Gabriel) **31, 32, 33**
jihad **95–7**
judgement **20, 36, 37–9**
Jummah prayer **84**
justice **19, 23**

K

Ka'bah **92, 93**
Karbala **99, 100**
khalifah (caliph) **16**
khitan **55, 56**
Khums **89, 90–1**
kiraman katibin ('noble scribes') **31, 33, 37**
Kitab al-iman **16, 18**
kutubullah **28**

L

Laylat al-Qadr (Night of Power) **85, 87–8**
legal system (shari'ah) **56**
lesser jihad **95, 96–7**
life after death **37–40, 119–25**
life, sanctity of **111–12, 118**
Lot **50**

M

Makkah (Mecca) **92, 93**
malaikah (angels) **31–3**
marriage **47–8, 49, 52, 61–3**
martyrs **97**
mediums **124**
men, role of **64, 65–6**
  see also equality of men and women
mercy **22–3**
Mi'ad **19, 20**
Mika'il (Michael) **32–3**
miracles **24, 26**
Moses **26, 28**
mosques
  in Britain **13**
  community role **56, 57**

prayer **55, 69, 83–4**
  women as prayer leaders **69**
Muhammad
  equality of men and women **65**
  marriage **47, 52**
  Night of Power **87–8**
  prophethood **24, 27**
  and Qur'an **29**
  as role model **27, 64**
  Salah **82**
  servant and messenger of Allah **17, 27, 80**
  succession disagreement **16**
Musa (Moses) **26, 28**

N

Nahi anil munkar **77, 78**
natural resources **129**
natural world **129–30**
Night of Power **85, 87–8**
nikah **47**
nisab **89**
Nubuwwah (prophethood) **19, 24–7, 80**
nuclear families **53**

O

omnipotence **21, 22**
omniscience **34**

P

paradise (jannah) **38, 124**
paranormal activity/beliefs **119, 120, 121**
parents **56**
pilgrimage **92–4**
political leadership **68**
pollution **129**
prayer **69, 82–4**
predestination **34–6**
prejudice **67–70**
premarital sex **49, 50**
pro-choice **116, 117**
pro-life **116, 117**
procreation **47, 53**
prophethood **19, 24–7, 80**
Psalms **28, 29**

Q

al-Qadr (predestination) **34–6**
qiblah **83, 84**
Qur'an **16–17, 21–3, 29–30**
  adultery **50**
  afterlife **119, 122**
  angels **32, 33**
  creation **108, 110**
  equality of men and women **67–8**
  human life, origins of **114**
  jihad **95, 96**
  life after death **119, 122**
  marriage **48, 62**
  men's role **64, 65–6**
  remarriage **62**
  sanctity of life **111**
  and science **109**
  sexual relationships **49, 50**
  women's role **65–6**

R

radicalism **97**
rak'ah **83, 84**
Ramadan **85–8**
recitations **83**
reincarnation **119, 120, 121**
remarriage **61, 62, 63**
resurrection **37**
revelation **28**
Risalah (prophethood) **24–7, 80**
rituals **55–6**

S

sadaqah (charity) **89**
Sahifah **28**
Salah **82–4**
same-sex parents **54**
sanctity of life **111–12, 118**
sawm (fasting) **85–8**
science **107, 109, 113–15**
scriptures **24, 26, 28**
  see also Qur'an
self-defence **96–7**
Sevener Shi'a Muslims **20**
sexual relationships **49–51**
Shahadah **79–81**
shari'ah (legal system) **56**

Shi'a Muslims
  Adalat **19**, **23**
  akhirah **40**
  Ashura **99–100**
  commemorations **100**
  Five Pillars of Islam **79**
  Hadith **16**
  Id-ul-Ghadeer **99**
  Khums **90–1**
  percentage of ummah **13**
  prayer **82**
  predestination **36**
  Sevener Shi'a Muslims **20**
  Ten Obligatory Acts **77–8**
  Twelver Shi'a Muslims **20**, **91**
  'Usul ad-Din, five roots of **19–20**
shirk (forbidden beliefs) **79**, **80**
sin **21**
Singer, Peter **132**
single-parent families **53–4**
situation ethics **59**, **60**, **63**, **118**, **127**
six Beliefs of Islam **16–18**
social welfare **89–90**
stewardship **129**
Sunni Muslims
  akhirah **40**
  commemorations **100**
  Five Pillars of Islam **79**
  Hadith **16**, **18**
  Khums **90**
  percentage of ummah **13**
  prayer **82**
  Ten Obligatory Acts **77**
surah **21**, **22**
surrogacy **53**, **54**
survival of the fittest **113**

T

tawaf **92**, **93**
Tawhid **19**, **21**, **80**
Tawrat (Torah) **28**
taxation, religious **89–91**
Ten Obligatory Acts **77–8**
terrorism **13**, **97**
Torah **28**
transcendence **21–2**
Twelver Shi'a Muslims **20**, **91**

U

ummah **13**, **53**, **55**
United Kingdom
  Islam in **13**
  marriage **48**
  religious beliefs **12**
universe, origins of **107–10**
'Usul ad-Din, five roots of **19–20**
utilitarianism **129**, **132**

W

war **96–7**
washing **82**, **84**
women
  pilgrimage **93**
  political leadership **68**
  prayer leading **69**
  role of **65–6**
  see also equality of men and women
worship **55**
  see also prayer
wudu' (ritual cleansing) **82**, **84**

Z

Zabur (Psalms) **28**, **29**
Zakah **89–90**, **91**

Acknowledgements

We are grateful to the authors and publishers for use of extracts from their titles and in particular for the following:

Excerpts from **The Qur'an OWC** translated by M. A. S. Abdel Haleem (Oxford University Press, 2008). © M. A. S. Abdel Haleem 2004, 2005. Reproduced with permission from Oxford University Press.

M. T. Ahmad, *An Elementary Study of Islam*, (Islam International Publications Ltd, 1996). Reproduced with permission from Islam International Publications Ltd.

M. T. Ahmad, *Revelation, Rationality, Knowledge and Truth*, (Islam International Publications Ltd, 1998). Reproduced with permission from Islam International Publications Ltd.

Ahmadiyya Muslim Youth Association: *Muslim Youth Group on Course to Plant 100,000 Trees*, 28th November 2014 (AMYA, 2014). Reproduced with permission from Ahmadiyya Muslim Youth Association UK.

M. Ahmedi: quote, (M. Ahmedi, 2016). Reproduced with permission from M. Ahmedi.

N. Allen: quote, (N. Allen, 2016). Reproduced with permission from N. Allen.

H. Almosawi: quote, (H. Almosawi, 2016). Reproduced with permission from H. Almosawi.

Anonymous: *Consciousness – Two Babies Talking in the Womb…*, http://thebacajourney.com/two-babies-talking-in-the-womb/ inspired by the short story 'Boy and Girl' from "Morphogeny", Copyright © Pablo J. Luis Molinero, 1980. All Rights reserved. Adaptation reproduced with permission from P. J. Luis Molinero and L. Seymour.

Artists for Israel International: *The Orthodox Jewish Bible*, fourth edition, (Artists for Israel International, 2011) © Copyright 2002, 2003, 2008, 2010, 2011 Artists for Israel International   All Rights Reserved Worldwide. 1st through 3rd Editions OJBC © 1996, 1997, 2003, 2008 Artists for Israel International. Reproduced with permission from Artists for Israel International.

Birmingham Central Mosque: *Services*, http://centralmosque.org.uk/default.aspx (Birmingham Central Mosque, 2016). Reproduced with permission from Birmingham Central Mosque.

British Humanist Association: *A humanist discussion of… Abortion*, http://humanismforschools.org.uk/pdfs/Abortion%20(final).pdf, (British Humanist Association, 2016). Reproduced with permission from the British Humanist Association.

I. Campbell: quote, (I. Campbell, 2016). Reproduced with permission from I. Campbell.

P. Covington: quote, (P. Covington, 2016). Reproduced with permission from P. Covington.

R. Dawkins: *The Problem with God: Interview with Richard Dawkins*, http://www.beliefnet.com/news/science-religion/2005/11/the-problem-with-god-interview-with-richard-dawkins.aspx? (Beliefnet, 2016). Reproduced with permission from R. Dawkins.

Z. Hussain: quote, (Z. Hussain, 2016). Reproduced with permission from Z. Hussain.

S. Khatun: quote, (S. Khatun, 2016). Reproduced with permission from S. Khatun.

Dr I. Masood: quote, (Dr I. Masood, 2016). Reproduced with permission from Dr Masood.

Roshni Nair: *While the revolution gently weeps: An interview with Mona Eltahawy*, dna, 1st Nov 2015, (dna, 2015). Reproduced with permission from dna, diligent media coroperation.

P. Singer: *Practical Ethics*, (Cambridge University Press, 2011). © Peter Singer 1980, 1993, 2011. Reproduced with permission from Cambridge University Press.

K. Warby: quote, (K. Warby, 2016). Reproduced with permission from K. Warby.

Dr. A. Wadud: quote, 17th October 2008 (A. Wadud, 2008). Reproduced with permission from Dr Wadud.

D. Webster: quote, (D. Webster, 2016). Reproduced with permission from D. Webster.

A. A. Zaidi: quote, (A. A. Zaidi, 2016). Reproduced with permission from A. A. Zaidi.

The publishers would like to thank the following for permission to use their photographs:

COVER: ImagesBazaar/Getty Images

Specification mapping and revision page backgrounds: mironov/Shutterstock

p4: Lolostock / Shutterstock; **p6**: Photoonlife / Shutterstock; **p7**: totallypic / Shutterstock; **p8**: Nikolaeva / Shutterstock; **p9**: SH-Vector / Shutterstock; **p10**: Tang Yan Song / Shutterstock; **p11**: Sutichak / Shutterstock; **p12**: Samuel E. Shropshire / www.samslifeinjeddah.wordpress.com; **p13**: Jamie Jones/REX/Shutterstock; **p13**: Angelo Hornak/Corbis via Getty Images; **p13**: Tanveer Khokhar; **p13**: Catriona Robertson; **p14**: Zurijeta / Shutterstock; **p17**: Gyuszko-Photo / Shutterstock; **p18**: By Ian Miles-Flashpoint Pictures / Alamy Stock Photo; **p19**: DNY59 / iStock; **p20**: Leader.ir - Pool/Anadolu Agency/Getty Images; **p21**: Shutterstock; **p22**: Eliza Snow / iStock; **p23**: Eric Meola / Corbis; **p25**: Valentin Valkov / Shutterstock; **p25**: Zurijeta / Shutterstock; **p26**: Benny Marty / Shutterstock; **p27**: Rahhal / Shutterstock; **p28**: eldinhoid / iStock; **p29**: PhotosIndia.com LLC / Alamy Stock Photo; **p30**: Stringer/Anadolu Agency/Getty Images; **p32**: Lenar Musin/Shutterstock; **p33**: ZUMA Press, Inc./Alamy; **p34**: destinacigdem / 123RF; **p35**: Samuel Borges Photography / Shutterstock; **p36**: hikrcn / Shutterstock; **p36**: Zameer Hussain; **p37**: BANARAS KHAN/AFP/Getty Images; **p38**: Ditty_about_summer / Shutterstock; **p39**: Hadi Y Djunaedi / 123RF; **p39**: DNY59 / iStock; **p40**: Zameer Hussain; **p40**: Shelina Khatun; **p45**: oliveromg / Shutterstock; **p47**: Muzmatch.com; **p49**: Megapress / Alamy Stock Photo; **p50**: Catchlight Visual Services / Alamy Stock Photo; **p51**: David M. Benett/Getty Images; **p51**: Janine Wiedel/REX/Shutterstock; **p52**: Yuri_Arcurs / iStock; **p53**: Zurijeta / Shutterstock; **p53**: epa european pressphoto agency b.v. / Alamy Stock Photo; **p54**: Jamie McCarthy/Getty Images; **p55**: Jamie Jones/REX/Shutterstock; **p55**: Ezz Mika Elya / Shutterstock; **p56**: AFP/Getty Images; **p57**: Rui Vieira / PA Archive/Press Association Images; **p58**: lion Photos / Shutterstock; **p59**: Phanie / Alamy Stock Photo; **p60**: Art Directors & TRIP / Alamy Stock Photo; **p61**: Photographee.eu / Shutterstock; **p62**: Sneksy / iStock; **p63**: Peter Covington; **p64**: Arie Arie Toursino Hadi / Alamy Stock Photo; **p65**: Chris Schmidt / Getty Images; **p65**: oliveromg / Shutterstock; **p66**: Kymberley Warby; **p67**: Fotosearch / Getty Images; **p68**: kzenon / iStock; **p68**: Francis Dean/REX/Shutterstock; **p69**: epa european pressphoto agency b.v. / Alamy Stock Photo; **p70**: www.imamsonline.com; **p75**: hikrcn/Shutterstock; **p75**: NOAH SEELAM / Stringer / Getty Images; **p78**: Sorin Vidis / Shutterstock; **p79**: author; **p79**: ANURAK PONGPATIMET/Shutterstock; **p80**: Q2A media; **p80**: Debby Wong/Shutterstock; **p81**: author; **p81**: © Gregg Vignal / Alamy Stock Photo; **p82**: AfricaImages/iStock; **p83**: IS_ImageSource/iStock; **p84**: author; **p85**: baibaz/Shutterstock; **p86**: author; **p87**: epa european pressphoto agency b.v. / Alamy Stock Photo; **p88**: hikrcn/Shutterstock; **p88**: AFP/Stringer/Getty Images; **p89**: Elnur/Shutterstock; **p90**: Spencer Platt/Staff/Getty Images; **p91**: khwanchai.s/Shutterstock; **p92**: FAYEZ NURELDINE/Staff/ Getty Images; **p93**: © JTB MEDIA CREATION, Inc. / Alamy Stock Photo; **p93**: Dilek Mermer/Anadolu Agency/Getty Images; **p94**: Bilal Randeree; **p94**: © Everett Collection Historical / Alamy Stock Photo; **p95**: © BSIP SA / Alamy Stock Photo; **p96**: IS_ImageSource/iStock; **p96**: Photographee.eu/Shutterstock; **p96**: Gajus/Shutterstock; **p96**: www.myjihad.org; **p96**: © Tommy Trenchard / Alamy Stock Photo; **p98**: NOAH SEELAM / Stringer / Getty Images; **p99**: © Janine Wiedel Photolibrary / Alamy Stock Photo; **p99**: © Ehsan Ahmad/Demotix/Corbis; **p100**: © epa european pressphoto agency b.v. / Alamy Stock Photo; **p105**: Igor Zh. / Shutterstock; **p105**: John Birdsall/REX/Shutterstock; **p107**: Igor Zh. / Shutterstock; **p108**: Antares_StarExplorer / Shutterstock; **p109**: Keystone/Getty Images; **p109**: Dr Imran Masood; **p113**: Classic Image / Alamy Stock Photo; **p114**: LIONEL BRET/LOOK AT SCIENCES/SCIENCE PHOTO LIBRARY; **p115**: Getty Images/National Geographic Creative; **p116**: DR NAJEEB LAYYOUS/SCIENCE PHOTO LIBRARY; **p117**: Jim West / Alamy Stock Photo; **p117**: B Christopher / Alamy Stock Photo; **p119**: DEA PICTURE LIBRARY/De Agostini/Getty Images; **p120**: Anatoleya / Getty Images; **p120**: Irita Campbell; **p120**: ShaunWilkinson / Shutterstock; **p122**: Orgus88 / Shutterstock; **p123**: Geraint Lewis / Alamy Stock Photo; **p123**: Dr David Webster / www.davewebster.org; **p124**: CHARLES OMMANNEY/REX/Shutterstock; **p125**: CLIPAREA I Custom media / Shutterstock; **p126**: Rob Stothard/Getty Images; **p127**: Juanmonino / iStock; p128: John Birdsall/REX/Shutterstock; p129: Fotos593 / Shutterstock; **p130**: Ahmadiyya Muslim Youth Association UK / www.muslimsforhumanity.org.uk; **p130**: Eye Ubiquitous/REX/Shutterstock; **p131**: Olga Kolos / Alamy Stock Photo

We have made every effort to trace and contact all copyright holders before publication, but if notified of any errors or omissions the publisher will rectify these at the earliest opportunity.

Thank you to James Helling for the index.